Contract Law
2010–2011

Routledge
Taylor & Francis Group

LONDON AND

Seventh edition published 2010
by Routledge
2 Park Square, Milton Park, Abingdon, Oxon OX14 4RN

Simultaneously published in the USA and Canada
by Routledge
270 Madison Avenue, New York, NY 10016

Routledge is an imprint of the Taylor & Francis Group, an informa business

© 2006, 2008, 2010 Routledge

Previous editions published by Cavendish Publishing Limited
First edition   1997
Second edition   1999
Third edition   2002
Fourth edition   2004

Typeset in Rotis by RefineCatch Limited, Bungay, Suffolk
Printed and bound in Great Britain by TJ International Ltd, Padstow, Cornwall

British Library Cataloguing in Publication Data
A catalogue record for this book is available from the British Library

Library of Congress Control Number: 2009912618

ISBN-10: 0–415–56660–6 (pbk)
ISBN-13: 978–0–415–56660–5 (pbk)

ISBN-10: 0–203–85797–6 (eBook)
ISBN-13: 978–0–203–85795–3 (eBook)

Contents

Table of Cases

Table of Statutes

Table of European Legislation

Table of Statutory Instruments

How to use this book

Welcome to this new edition of Routledge Contract Law Lawcards. In response to student feedback, we've added some new features to these new editions to give you all the support and preparation you need in order to face your law exams with confidence.

Inside this book you will find:

▨ NEW tables of cases and statutes for ease of reference

■ Revision Checklists

We've summarised the key topics you will need to know for your law exams and broken them down into a handy revision checklist. Check them out at the beginning of each chapter, then after you have the chapter down, revisit the checklist and tick each topic off as you gain knowledge and confidence.

1

Sources of law

Primary legislation: Acts of Parliament	☐
Secondary legislation	☐
Case law	☐
System of precedent	☐
Common law	☐
Equity	☐
EU law	☐
Human Rights Act 1998	☐

■ Key Cases

We've identified the key cases that are most likely to come up in exams. To help you to ensure that you can cite cases with ease, we've included a brief account of the case and judgment for a quick aide-memoire.

■ Companion Website

HENDY LENNOX v GRAHAME PUTTICK [1984]

Basic facts

Diesel engines were supplied, subject to a *Romalpa* clause, then fitted to generators. Each engine had a serial number. When the buyer became insolvent the seller sought to recover one engine. The Receiver argued that the process of fitting the engine to the generator passed property to the buyer. The court disagreed and allowed the seller to recover the still identifiable engine despite the fact that some hours of work would be required to disconnect it.

Relevance

If the property remains identifiable and is not irredeemably changed by the manufacturing process a *Romalpa* clause may be viable.

At the end of each chapter you will be prompted to visit the Routledge Lawcards companion website where you can test your understanding online with specially prepared multiple-choice questions, as well as revise the key terms with our online glossary.

You should now be confident that you would be able to tick all of the boxes on the checklist at the beginning of this chapter. To check your knowledge of Sources of law why not visit the companion website and take the Multiple Choice Question test. Check your understanding of the terms and vocabulary used in this chapter with the flashcard glossary.

◼ Exam Practice

Once you've acquired the basic knowledge, you'll want to put it to the test. The Routledge Questions and Answers provides examples of the kinds of questions that you will face in your exams, together with suggested answer plans and a fully-worked model answer. We've included one example free at the end of this book to help you put your technique and understanding into practice.

QUESTION 1

What are the main sources of law today?

Answer plan

This is, apparently, a very straightforward question, but the temptation is to ignore the European Community (EU) as a source of law and to over-emphasise custom as a source. The following structure does not make these mistakes:

◼ in the contemporary situation, it would not be improper to start with the EU as a source of UK law;

◼ then attention should be moved on to domestic sources of law: statute and common law;

◼ the increased use of delegated legislation should be emphasised;

◼ custom should be referred to, but its extremely limited operation must be emphasised.

ANSWER

European law

Since the UK joined the European Economic Community (EEC), now the EU, it has progressively but effectively passed the power to create laws which are operative in this country to the wider European institutions. The UK is now subject to Community law, not just as a direct consequence of the various treaties of accession passed by the UK Parliament, but increasingly, it is subject to the secondary legislation generated by the various institutions of the EU.

1

Agreement

The traditional view that an agreement requires the identification of a valid offer and a valid acceptance of that offer has been challenged in recent years by:

- Lord Denning in *Gibson v Manchester City Council* [1979] and *Butler Machine Tool Co Ltd v Ex-Cell-O Corpn Ltd* [1979] where he stated that providing the parties were agreed on all material points, then there was no need for the traditional analysis;

- Lord Justice Steyn (*obiter*) in *Trentham Ltd v Archital Luxfer* [1993] where he stated that a strict analysis of offer and acceptance was not necessary in an executed contract in a commercial setting.

The traditional view, however, was applied by the HOL in *Gibson v Manchester City Council* [1979].

Lord Diplock did recognise that there may be some 'exceptional contracts which do not fit easily into an analysis of offer and acceptance', for example, a multi-partite contract as in *Clarke v Dunraven* [1897], but he stressed that in most contracts the 'conventional' approach of seeking an offer and an acceptance of that offer must be adhered to.

In normal cases, therefore, a valid offer and a valid acceptance of that offer must be identified.

A **bilateral agreement** consists of an exchange of promises, for example:

Offer – I will sell my car for £500

Acceptance – I will give you £500 for your car

In a **unilateral agreement** the offeror alone makes a promise in return for an act. The offer is accepted by doing what is set out in the offer, for example:

Offer – I will pay £500 to anyone who returns my lost kitten

Acceptance – The lost kitten is returned

UNILATERAL AND BILATERAL AGREEMENTS

The distinction is important with regard to:

- advertisements;

■ revocation of offers;

■ communication of acceptance.

OFFER

> A definite promise to be bound provided that certain specified terms are accepted

A valid offer:

■ must be communicated, so that the offeree may accept or reject it;

■ may be communicated in writing, orally, or by conduct;

(There is no general requirement that an agreement must be in writing. Important exceptions include contracts relating to interests in land (Law of Property (Miscellaneous Provisions) Act 1989, s 2(1)), and consumer credit (Consumer Credit Act 1974).)

■ may be made to a particular person, to a group of persons, or to the whole world.

▶ CARLILL v CARBOLIC SMOKE BALL CO LTD [1893]

Facts

The defendants issued an advertisement in which they offered to pay £100 to any person who used their smoke balls and then succumbed to influenza. Mrs Carlill saw the advertisement and used the smoke ball, but then immediately caught influenza. She sued for the £100. The defendants argued that it was not possible in English law to make an offer to the whole world.

Held

Mrs Carlill had a valid contract. An offer can be made to the whole world (unilateral contract).

The offer:

■ must be definite in substance (see certainty of terms, below).

▦ must be distinguished from an invitation to treat.

INVITATIONS TO TREAT

> An indication that the invitor is willing to enter into negotiations but is not prepared to be bound immediately

▶ GIBSON v MANCHESTER CITY COUNCIL [1979]

A completed application form will usually be construed as an invitation to treat.

Facts

MCC were prepared to sell council properties to sitting tenants.

The council's letter stated 'we may be prepared to sell you . . .'. Gibson completed an application form which accompanied the letter. HOL had to decide whether the council's letter constituted an offer.

Held

The original letter was an invitation to treat, thus no contract had been created.

A response to an invitation to treat does not lead to an agreement. The response may, however, be an offer.

The distinction between an offer and an invitation to treat depends on the objectively determined intentions of the parties.

The courts have established that there is no intention to be bound in the following cases:

Display of goods for sale

▦ In a shop.

▶ PHARMACEUTICAL SOCIETY OF GB v BOOTS CASH CHEMISTS LTD [1953]

The display of goods in a shop is an invitation to treat. The offer is made when the customer presents the goods to the shopkeeper at the checkout.

Facts

Boots Cash Chemists changed one of their shops to a self-service outlet. The Pharmacy and Poisons Act 1933 specified that certain drugs and poisons should not be sold other than **under the supervision of a registered pharmacist**. In order to interpret whether or not an offence had been committed, the Court had to decide when the contract had been formed.

Held

The contract was formed when the item was presented at the cash desk. At this point a pharmacist was present so no offence had been committed.

▓ In a shop window.

▶ FISHER v BELL [1961]

Facts

A shopkeeper was prosecuted under the Offensive Weapons Act 1959 for 'offering for sale' an offensive weapon. The shopkeeper was displaying a flick knife with a price attached in the window.

Held

The display of the flick knife was an invitation to treat, rather than an offer, thus the shopkeeper was found not guilty of the offence.

However, it was suggested by Lord Denning in *Thornton v Shoe Lane Parking* [1971] (see below) that vending machines and automatic ticket machines are making offers since, once the money has been inserted, the transaction is irrevocable.

- In an advertisement.

▶ PARTRIDGE v CRITTENDEN [1968]

An advertisement in a newspaper or magazine will constitute an invitation to treat.

Facts

The defendant was prosecuted under the Protection of Birds Act 1954 for offering for sale a wild bird. The advertisement read: 'Bramble-finch cocks and hens – 25s'.

Held

The advertisement was held to be an invitation to treat. The court pointed out that, if the advertisement was treated as an offer, this could lead to many actions for breach of contract against the advertiser, as his stock of birds was limited. He could not have intended the advertisement to be an offer.

However, if the advertisement is unilateral in nature, and there is no problem of limited stock, then it may be an offer. See *Carlill v Carbolic Smoke Ball Co Ltd* (above). Advertising a reward may also be a unilateral offer.

Auctions

- An auctioneer's request for bids in *Payne v Cave* [1789] was held to be an invitation to treat. The offer was made by the bidder (cf Sale of Goods Act 1979, s 57(2)).

- A notice of an auction. In *Harris v Nickerson* [1873], it was held that a notice that an auction would be held on a certain date was not an offer which then could be accepted by turning up at the stated time. It was a statement of intention.

If the auction is stated to be 'without reserve', then there is still no necessity to hold an auction, but, if the auction is held, lots must be sold to the highest bidder (*Barry v Heathcote Ball* [2001]), confirming *obiter dicta* in *Warlow v Harrison* [1859]). The phrase 'without reserve' constitutes a unilateral offer which can be accepted by turning up and submitting the highest bid.

Tenders

A request for tenders is normally an invitation to treat.

▨ However, it was held in *Harvela Ltd v Royal Trust of Canada* [1985] that if the request is made to specified parties and it is stated that the contract will be awarded to the lowest or the highest bidder, then this will be binding as an implied unilateral offer. It was also held in that case that a referential bid, for example, 'the highest other bid plus 10%' was not a valid bid.

▨ It was also held in *Blackpool and Fylde Aero Club v Blackpool BC* [1990] that, if the request is addressed to specified parties, this amounts to a unilateral offer that consideration will be given to each tender which is properly submitted.

▶ BLACKPOOL AND FYLDE AERO CLUB v BLACKPOOL BOROUGH COUNCIL [1990]

Where a party has issued an invitation to tender, it is bound to consider all correctly submitted tenders

Facts

Blackpool BC invited tenders from people who were interested in operating leisure flights from the local airfield. Tenders had to be submitted to the Town Hall by a stated deadline. The Aero Club submitted its application on time but the Council refused to consider it, as due to an error on their part, they mistakenly believed that the tender had been submitted after the deadline.

Held

COA held that the council's invitation to tender was a unilateral offer to consider all tenders which fell within its rules. The tender constituted an offer which had been accepted by the Aero Club. The offer was accepted by any party who put in a tender. Thus the council were obliged to consider all tenders (acceptances) to their offer, including the Aero Club tender. They were not of course obliged to accept the tender.

SUBJECT TO CONTRACT

The words 'subject to contract' may be placed on top of a letter in order to indicate that an offer is not to be legally binding (*Walford v Miles* [1992]).

TERMINATION OF THE OFFER

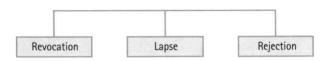

REVOCATION (TERMINATION BY THE OFFEROR)

An offeror may withdraw an offer at any time before it has been accepted.

■ The revocation must be communicated to the offeree before acceptance.

> **▶ BYRNE v VAN TIENHOVEN [1880]**
>
> **Withdrawal of an offer by telegram will be valid when it is received.**
>
> *Facts*
>
> VT (in Cardiff) wrote to B (in New York) on 1 October offering certain goods for sale. VT sent a letter withdrawing the offer on 8 October. B received the initial offer letter on 11 October and accepted by telegram. The revocation letter of 8 October was then received on 20 October.
>
> *Held*
>
> There was a valid contract in place when B accepted the offer on 11 October. The revocation letter of 8 October was ineffective as it was received **after** acceptance had taken place.

■ Communication need not be made by the offeror; communication through a third party will suffice. In *Dickinson v Dodds* [1876], the plaintiff was told by a neighbour that a property which had been offered to him had been sold to a third party. Held – the offer had been validly revoked.

■ An offer to keep an offer open for a certain length of time can be withdrawn like any other unless an option has been purchased, for example, consideration has been given to keep the offer open (*Routledge v Grant* [1828]).

Unilateral offers

▨ Communication of the revocation is difficult if the offer was to the whole world. It was suggested, however, in the American case of *Shuey v USA* [1875] that communication will be assumed if the offeror takes reasonable steps to inform the public, for example, places an advertisement in the same newspaper.

▨ It now seems established that revocation cannot take place if the offeree has started to perform.

▶ ERRINGTON v ERRINGTON [1952]

Facts

A father promised his daughter and son-in-law that, if they paid off the mortgage on a house he owned, he would give it to them. The young couple duly paid the instalments, but the offer was withdrawn shortly before the whole debt was paid.

Held

There was an implied term in the offer that it was irrevocable once performance had begun. This is also supported by *dicta* in *Daulia v Four Millbank Nominees* [1978].

LAPSE (TERMINATION BY OPERATION OF LAW)

An offer may lapse and thus be incapable of being accepted because of:

▨ Passage of time:

● at the end of a stipulated time (if any); or

● if no time is stipulated, after a reasonable time.

In *Ramsgate Victoria Hotel Co v Montefiore* [1866], an attempt to accept an offer to buy shares after five months failed as the offer had clearly lapsed.

▨ Death:

● of the offeror if the offer was of a personal nature;

● of the offeree.

▨ Failure of a condition:

● an express condition; or

● an implied condition. In *Financings Ltd v Stimson* [1962], it was held that an offer to buy a car lapsed when the car was badly damaged on the ground that the offer contained an implied term that the car would remain in the same condition as when the offer was made.

REJECTION (TERMINATION BY THE OFFEREE)

A rejection may be:

▨ express;

▨ implied.

A counter offer is an implied rejection.

▨ Traditionally, an acceptance must be a mirror image of the offer. Any attempt by the offeree to change the terms of an offer will amount to a counter offer, and will terminate the original offer.

▶ HYDE v WRENCH [1840]

Facts

The defendant offered to sell a farm for £1,000. The plaintiff said he would give £950 for it, which was rejected by the defendant. The plaintiff later tried to accept the original offer price.

Held

The offer of £950 was a counter offer which terminated the original offer. The original offer was therefore no longer open for acceptance.

▶ BROGDEN v METROPOLITAN RAILWAY [1877]

Facts

The defendant sent to the plaintiff for signature a written agreement which they had negotiated. The plaintiff signed the agreement and entered in the name of an arbitrator on a space which had been left empty for this purpose.

Held

The returned document was not an acceptance but a counter offer. However acceptance was found to have taken place after the parties had conducted their business under the terms of the contract.

This is particularly important for businesses who contract by means of sales forms and purchase forms; for example, if an order placed by the buyer's purchase form is 'accepted' on the seller's sales form, and the conditions on the back of the two forms are not identical (which they are very unlikely to be), then the 'acceptance' is a counter offer and an implied rejection.

▶ BUTLER MACHINE TOOL CO LTD v EX–CELL–O CORPN LTD [1979]

Facts

The sellers offered to sell a machine tool to the buyers for £75,535 on their own conditions of sale which were stated to prevail over any conditions in the buyers' order form, and which contained a price variation clause. The buyers 'accepted' the offer on their own order form which stated that the price was a fixed price, and which contained a tear-off slip which said 'we accept your order on the terms and conditions stated thereon'. This was in effect a 'counter offer'. The sellers signed and returned the slip together with a letter which stated that they were carrying out the order in accordance with their original offer. When they delivered the machine, they claimed the price had increased by £2,892. The buyers refused to pay the extra sum.

Held

The contract was concluded on the buyers' terms; the signing and returning of the tear-off slip was conclusive that the sellers had accepted the buyers' counter offer. The court analysed the transaction by looking for matching offer and acceptance.

Note – a request for further information is not a counter offer.

> ### ❱ STEVENSON v McLEAN [1880]

Facts

The defendant offered to sell to the plaintiff iron at 40s a ton. The plaintiff telegraphed to inquire whether he could pay by instalments. The defendant did not reply and the plaintiff telegraphed again to accept the offer, at which time the defendant had sold the iron to a third party.

Held

The request to pay by instalments was a mere inquiry for information, not a counter offer. The original offer was therefore not rejected, and was still open when the plaintiff telegraphed his acceptance.

A CONDITIONAL ACCEPTANCE

A conditional acceptance may be a counter offer capable of acceptance, for example, I will pay £500 for your car if you paint it red. If the owner agrees to this condition, a contract will be formed.

ACCEPTANCE

The fact of acceptance | Communication of acceptance

THE FACT OF ACCEPTANCE

> An acceptance is a final and unqualified assent to all the terms of the offer

A valid acceptance must:

▪ be made while the offer is still in force (see termination of offer, above);

- be made by the offeree;

- exactly match the terms of the offer (see counter offers, above);

- be written, oral, or implied from conduct. In *Brogden v Metropolitan Railway* [1877] (above), the returned document was held to be a counter offer which the defendants then accepted either by ordering coal from Brogden or by accepting delivery of the coal.

However, the offeror may require the acceptance to be made in a certain way. If the requirement is mandatory, it must be followed.

> ▶ MANCHESTER DIOCESAN COUNCIL FOR EDUCATION v COMMERCIAL AND GENERAL INVESTMENTS LTD [1969]
>
> Facts
> An invitation to tender stated that the person whose bid was accepted would be informed by a letter to the address given in the tender. The acceptance was eventually sent not to this address but to the defendant's surveyor.
>
> Held
> The statement in the tender was not mandatory; the tender had therefore been validly accepted.

- Where the offer is made in alternative terms, the acceptance must make it clear to which set of terms it relates.

- A person cannot accept an offer of which he has no knowledge (*R v Clarke* [1927] (Australia)). But, a person's motive in accepting the offer is irrelevant.

> ▶ WILLIAMS v CARWARDINE [1833] (Australia)
>
> Facts
> The plaintiff knew of the offer of a reward in exchange for information on the identities of certain persons who had committed a murder. The plaintiff's motive for giving the information was to salve her conscience.

Held

The plaintiff was entitled to the reward.

■ 'Cross-offers' do not constitute an agreement (*Tinn v Hoffman & Co* [1873]).

COMMUNICATION OF ACCEPTANCE

Acceptance must be communicated

Acceptance must be communicated by the offeree or his agent. In *Powell v Lee* [1908], an unauthorised communication by one of the managers that the Board of Managers had selected a particular candidate for a headship was held not to be a valid acceptance.

Silence as communication

An offeror may not stipulate that silence of the offeree is to amount to acceptance.

▶ FELTHOUSE v BINDLEY [1862]

Facts

The plaintiff wrote to his nephew offering to buy a horse, and adding, 'If I hear no more . . . I will take it that the horse is mine'. The nephew did not reply to this letter.

Held

No contract. Acceptance had not been communicated to the offeror.

It has been suggested that this does not mean that silence can never amount to acceptance; for example, if, in *Felthouse v Bindley*, the offeree had relied on the offeror's statement that he need not communicate his acceptance, and wished to claim acceptance on that basis, the court could decide that the need for acceptance had been waived by the offeror (see below).

Unsolicited Goods

Where a company sends goods to a customer who has not requested them and then demands payment if the goods are not returned or rejected within a specified time limit, a consumer can treat the goods as an unconditioned gift as soon as they are received – Reg 24 Consumer Protection (Distance Selling Regulations) 2000.

Exceptions to the rule that acceptance must be communicated

- In a unilateral contract where communication is expressly or impliedly waived (see *Carlill v Carbolic Smoke Ball Co Ltd* (above)).

- Possibly where failure of communication is the fault of the offeror. This was suggested by Lord Denning in *Entores Ltd v Miles Far East Corpn* [1955].

- Where the post is deemed to be the proper method of communication.

▶ ADAMS v LINDSELL [1818]

Facts

The defendants wrote to the plaintiffs on 2 September offering to sell them a quantity of wool and requiring acceptance by post. The letter was incorrectly addressed and was received on 5 September. The plaintiffs immediately posted an acceptance on the same day which reached the defendants on 9 September. If the initial letter had been addressed correctly, a reply should have been received on 7 September. Unfortunately, having not received an acceptance the defendant sold the wool to a third party on 8 September.

Held

The contract was completed on 5 September, on the date that the acceptance was posted.

THE POSTAL RULE

Acceptance takes place when a letter is posted, not when it is received

Adams v Lindsell [1818], above.

Acceptance is effective on posting, even when the letter is lost in the post.

> ▶ HOUSEHOLD FIRE INSURANCE CO LTD v GRANT [1879]
>
> Facts
> The defendant offered to buy shares in the plaintiff's company. A letter of allotment was posted to the defendant, but it never reached him.
>
> Held
> The contract was completed when the letter was posted.

Note the difference between acceptance and revocation of an offer by post:

● Acceptance of an offer takes place when a letter is posted.

● Revocation of an offer takes place when the letter is received.

Byrne v Van Tienhoven [1880], above.

Limitations to the postal rule

It only applies to acceptances, and not to any other type of communication (for example, an offer or a revocation).

It only applies to letters and telegrams. It does not apply to instantaneous methods of communication such as telex or, probably, fax or email.

It must be reasonable to use the post as the means of communication (for example, an offer by telephone or by fax might indicate that a rapid method of response was required).

Letters of acceptance must be properly addressed and stamped.

The rule is easily displaced, for example, it may be excluded by the offeror either expressly or impliedly. In *Holwell Securities Ltd v Hughes* [1974], it was excluded by the offeror requiring 'notice in writing'. It was also suggested by the court that the postal rule would not be used where it would lead to manifest inconvenience.

Query – can a letter of acceptance be cancelled by actual communication before the letter is delivered?

There is no direct English authority on this point.

Arguments against
Logic – once a letter is posted, the offer is accepted; there is no provision in law for revoking an acceptance.

▨ The 'logical' view is supported by the New Zealand case of *Wenckheim v Arndt* [1878] and the South African case of *A to Z Bazaars (Pty) Ltd v Minister of Agriculture* [1974].

Fairness –

▨ Cheshire argues that it would be unfair to the offeror, who would be bound as soon as the letter was posted, whereas the offeree could keep his options open.

Arguments for
There is some support for allowing recall in the Scottish case of *Countess of Dunmore v Alexander* [1830].

▨ It is argued that actual prior communication of rejection would not necessarily prejudice the offeror, who, by definition, will be unaware of the 'acceptance'.

▨ It is also argued that it would be absurd to insist on enforcing a contract when both parties have acted on the recall. This, however, could be interpreted as an agreement to discharge.

COMMUNICATION BY INSTANTANEOUS/ELECTRONIC MEANS

Acceptance takes place when and where the message is received

▨ The rules on telephones and telex were laid down in *Entores v Miles* (above) and confirmed in *Brinkibon Ltd v Stahag Stahl* [1983] where it was suggested that, during normal office hours, acceptance takes place when the message is printed out not when it is read. The HOL, however, accepted that communication by telex may not always be instantaneous, for example, when received at night or when the office is closed.

Lord Wilberforce stated:

'No universal rule could cover all such cases; they must be resolved by reference to the intention of the parties, by sound business practice, and in some cases, by a judgment of where the risk should lie.'

It has been suggested that a message sent outside business hours should be 'communicated' when it is expected that it would be read, for example, at the next opening of business. It is generally accepted that the same rules should apply to faxes and email as to telex.

There is no direct authority on telephone answering machines. It might well be argued that the presence of an answering machine indicates that communication is not instantaneous; there is a delay between sending and receiving messages. It would then follow that the basic rule should apply, that is, that acceptance must be communicated. Acceptance, therefore, would take place when the message is actually heard by the offeror.

E-Commerce. It would seem likely that the display of goods and prices on a website will be treated as an invitation to treat and not as an offer, since otherwise there might well be thousands of acceptances at the click of a button of an item erroneously priced at £3 which should have been priced at £30.

The European Electronic Commerce Directive (Directive 2000/31/EC) sets out formalities that must be followed to make legally binding contracts over the Internet. Article 10 requires service providers to provide certain technical information on steps to be followed and information to be provided during transaction input. Article 11 requires that the service provider electronically acknowledge receipt of an order without undue delay.

These elements were implemented in the UK under the Electronic Commerce (EC Directive) Regulations 2002 (SI2002/2013). Under the regulations, where a contract is to be concluded by electronic means a service provider shall provide to the recipient, clear, comprehensible and unambiguous information on the following:

(a)   the different technical steps to follow to conclude the contract;

(b)   whether the concluded contract will be filed by the service provider and whether it will be accessible;

(c)   the technical means for identifying and correcting input errors prior to the placing of the order; and

(d)   the languages offered for the conclusion of the contract.

Article 9 of the EC directive requires member states to ensure that their legal systems allow contracts to be concluded electronically (with a few minor exceptions). This is implemented in the UK under s 8 of the Electronic Communications Act 2000, which introduces a power to remove restrictions which have arisen where a current statute prohibits the use of electronic transactions. Part II of the 2000 Act also incorporates legal recognition of electronic signatures. Under the Act, an electronic contract is concluded when the buyer has received an acknowledgement that their acceptance has been received, and has confirmed receipt of that acknowledgement. The communications are effective when the receiving party is able to access them.

The Consumer Protection (Distance Selling) Regulations 2000 provide a consumer with a 7 day cooling-off period after the completion of certain contracts made at a distance. If the contract falls within these regulations, it can be cancelled during this 7 day period. The contract in question must have been made under an organised distance-selling arrangement, i.e. by post, internet or telephone. However, there are a large number of contracts that are excluded from protection, for example contracts for the sale of land, leisure, transport and the supply of food for consumption. So, if I purchase a train ticket or order a pizza from a fast food takeaway, these contracts will not benefit from the cooling-off provision.

CERTAINTY OF TERMS

However, the uncertainty may be cured by:

◼ a trade custom, where a word has a specific meaning;

◼ previous dealings between the parties whereby a word or phrase has acquired a specific meaning, for example, timber of 'fair specification' in *Hillas v Arcos* [1932];

◼ the contract itself, which provides a method for resolving an uncertainty. In

> It is for the parties to make their intentions clear

The courts will not enforce:

Vague agreements, for example:	**Incomplete agreements,** for example:
Scammell v Ouston [1941]	'an agreement to make an agreement' will be void, in *Walford v Miles* [1992], the court refused to enforce an 'agreement to negotiate in good faith'.
The courts refused to enforce a sale stated to be made 'on hire purchase terms', neither the rate of interest, nor the period of repayment, nor the number of instalments were stated.	See, also, *May and Butcher v R* [1934].

Foley v Classique Coaches [1934], there was an executed contract where the vagueness of 'at a price to be agreed' was cured by a provision in the contract referring disputes to arbitration. Cf *May and Butcher v R* [1934], an unexecuted contract, where the court refused to allow a similar arbitration clause to cure the uncertainty.

The courts will strive to find a contract valid where it has been executed.

- The Sale of Goods Act 1979 provides that if no price or mechanism for fixing the price is provided, then the buyer must pay a 'reasonable price', but this provision will not apply where the contract states that the price is 'to be agreed between the parties'.

- Note, a 'lock-out agreement', for example, an agreement not to negotiate with anyone else, is valid provided it is clearly stated and for a specific length of time. This was applied by the COA in *Pitt v PHH Asset Management* [1993] where a promise not to negotiate with any third party for two weeks was enforced.

You should now be confident that you would be able to tick all of the boxes on the checklist at the beginning of this chapter. To check your knowledge of Agreement why not visit the companion website and take the Multiple Choice Question test. Check your understanding of the terms and vocabulary used in this chapter with the flashcard glossary.

2

Consideration

Most legal systems will only enforce promises where there is something to indicate that the promisor intended to be bound, that is, there is some:

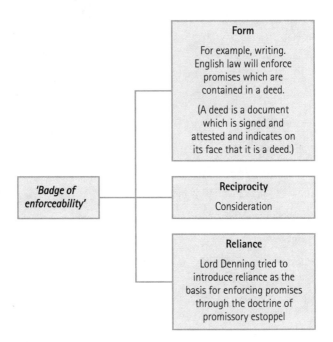

Form

For example, writing. English law will enforce promises which are contained in a deed.

(A deed is a document which is signed and attested and indicates on its face that it is a deed.)

'Badge of enforceability'

Reciprocity

Consideration

Reliance

Lord Denning tried to introduce reliance as the basis for enforcing promises through the doctrine of promissory estoppel

Consideration is the normal 'badge of enforceability' in English law.

DEFINITIONS OF CONSIDERATION

A valuable consideration in the eyes of the law may consist of the following (*Currie v Misa* [1875]):

- either some right, interest, profit or benefit to one party; or

- some forbearance, detriment, loss or responsibility given, suffered or undertaken by the other.

Shorter version:

> A benefit to one party or a detriment to the other

LIMITATION OF THE DEFINITION

▣ It makes no mention of why the promisee incurs a detriment or confers a benefit, or that the element of a bargain is central to the classical notion of consideration. For example, in *Combe v Combe* [1951], it was held that there was no consideration for the defendant's promise to pay his ex-wife £100 per year even though in reliance on that promise she had not applied to the divorce court for maintenance, and in that sense she had suffered a detriment. The reason why the detriment did not constitute consideration was that there was no request by the husband, express or implied, that she should forbear from applying for maintenance. There was no 'exchange'.

▣ Some writers have preferred to emphasise this element of bargain and have defined consideration as:

'the element of exchange in a contract'

or

'the price paid for a promise'

▣ These definitions, however, are vague and, despite its limitation, the benefit/ detriment definition is most commonly used.

CONSIDERATION AND CONDITION

Consideration must be distinguished from the fulfilment of a condition. If A says to B, 'I will give you £500 if you should break a leg', there is no contract but simply a gratuitous promise subject to a condition. In *Carlill v Carbolic Smoke Ball Co* [1893], the plaintiff provided consideration for the defendant's promise by using the smoke ball. Catching influenza was only a condition of her entitlement to enforce the promise.

KINDS OF CONSIDERATION

```
            ┌──────────────────┴──────────────────┐
┌───────────────────────────┐   ┌───────────────────────────┐
│   Executory consideration  │   │   Executed consideration   │
│      A promise to do       │   │    An act wholly performed  │
│   something in the future  │   │     as part of a contract   │
└───────────────────────────┘   └───────────────────────────┘
            ┌───────────────────────────────────────┐
            │ Past consideration, that is, something already │
            │ completed before the promise is made cannot    │
            │ generally amount to consideration              │
            └───────────────────────────────────────┘
```

A promise made after a contract has been entered into will not be enforceable as no consideration will have been provided for the promise.

▶ ROSCORLA v THOMAS [1842]

Facts

The defendant promised the plaintiff that a horse which had been bought by him was sound and free from vice.

Held

Since the promise was made after the sale had been completed, there was no consideration for it and it could not be enforced.

- In *Re McArdle* [1951], a promise made 'in consideration of your carrying out certain improvements to the property' was held by the COA to be unenforceable as all the work had been done before the promise was made.

Exceptions to this rule:

- The modern requirements were laid down by Lord Scarman in *Pau On v Lau Yiu Long* [1980]. Where a service is rendered:

  ● at the request of the promisor (as in *Lampleigh v Braithwait* [1615]);

  ● on the understanding that a payment will be made (as in *Re Casey's Patents* [1892]); and

● if the payment would have been legally enforceable if it had been promised in advance,

then a subsequent promise to pay a certain sum will be enforced.

Note – the 'inferred' intention to pay makes this a very flexible exception.

> PAO ON v LAU YIU LONG [1980]

An act done before the giving of a promise to make a payment or to confer some other benefit can sometimes be consideration for a promise

Facts

As part of a wider agreement, Pao On promised not to sell 60% of the shares they owned in Lau Yiu's company. Subsequently Lau Yiu agreed to buy back 2.5 million shares at a fixed price, to protect against losses if the value of the shares fluctuated. Pao On then realised that this was a bad bargain, because the value of the shares could increase. Pao On then refused to proceed with the first agreement unless Lau Yiu cancelled the 2nd agreement and replaced it with an indemnity which guaranteed a minimum of $2.5 per share. Lau Yiu provided the indemnity. The share value fell and Pao On claimed the money due under the indemnity. Lau Yiu refused.

Held

The promise by Pao On not to sell the shares was found to be good consideration for the guarantee. Although the promise had been made before the guarantee was given, it had been made at Lau Yiu's request and on the understanding that Pao On were, in return for making it, to receive some form of protection against the risk of a fall in the share value.

CONSIDERATION MUST MOVE FROM THE PROMISEE

Only a person who has provided consideration for a promise can enforce that promise

See Chapter 10 – Privity of contract.

CONSIDERATION NEED NOT BE ADEQUATE

> The consideration provided by one party need not equal in value the consideration provided by the other party

It is for the parties themselves to make their own bargain. The consideration need only have 'some value in the eyes of the law'. (See 'Consideration must be sufficient', p 29, below.)

The value may be slight. In *Chappell Co Ltd v Nestlé Co Ltd* [1960], three wrappers from the defendant's chocolate bars were held to be part of the consideration. In *Mountford v Scott* [1975], £1 was held to be good consideration for an option to buy a house.

Withdrawal of threatened legal proceedings will amount to consideration, even if the claim is found to have no legal basis, provided that the parties themselves believe that the claim is valid (*Callisher v Bischoffstein* [1870]).

In *Pitt v PHH Asset Management* [1993], the defendants agreed to a lock-out agreement in return for Pitt dropping his claim for an injunction against them. The claim for an injunction had no merit, but had a nuisance value, and dropping it was therefore good consideration.

In *Alliance Bank v Broome* [1964], the bank's forbearance to sue was held to be consideration for the defendant's promise to provide security for a loan.

In *Edmonds v Lawson* [2000] it was held that the general benefits to chambers of operating a pupillage system were sufficient to provide consideration for contracts with individual pupils.

There is no consideration, however, where the promises are vague, for example, 'to stop being a nuisance to his father' (*White v Bluett* [1853]; but cf *Ward v Byham* [1956], below) or illusory, for example, to do something impossible, or merely good, for example, to show love or affection or gratitude.

It has been argued that, because the latter are invalid, consideration must have some economic value. But, economic value is extremely difficult to discern in the other cases cited above. Since consideration is a 'badge of enforceability', it is argued that nominal consideration is adequate; it is only designed to show that the promise is intended to be legally enforceable – whether it creates any economic advantage is therefore irrelevant.

> Consideration, therefore, is found when a person receives whatever he requests in return for a promise whether or not it has an economic value, provided it is not too vague

CONSIDERATION MUST BE SUFFICIENT

> The consideration must have some value in the eyes of the law

Traditionally, the following have no value in the eyes of the law:

```
        ┌──────────────────────────┴──────────────────────────┐
┌───────────────────┐                          ┌─────────────────────────┐
│   Performing a     │                          │   Performing an existing │
│   duty imposed     │                          │   contractual duty owed  │
│   by law           │                          │   to the other party     │
└───────────────────┘                          └─────────────────────────┘
```

PERFORMING A DUTY IMPOSED BY LAW

- For example, promising not to commit a crime, or promising to appear in court after being subpoenaed.

▶ COLLINS v GODEFROY [1831]

Facts

The argument centred on a promise made by the defendant to pay a fee to a witness who had been properly subpoenaed to attend a trial.

Held

The promise had been made without consideration. The witness had a public duty to attend.

- If a person does, or promises to do, more than he is required to do by law, then he is providing consideration.

▶ GLASBROOK BROS v GLAMORGAN CC [1925]

Facts

The council, as police authority, on the insistence of a colliery owner, and in return for a promise of payment, provided protection over and above that required by law.

Held

They were able to enforce the promise, as their additional activities were deemed to constitute consideration for the promise of payment.

▶ WARD v BYHAM [1956]

Facts

The father of an illegitimate child promised to pay the mother an allowance of £1 per week if she proved that the child was 'well looked after and happy'.

Held

The mother was entitled to enforce the promise because in under-taking to see that the child was 'well looked after and happy', she was doing more than her legal obligation.

Lord Denning, however, based his decision on the ground that the mother provided consideration by performing her legal duty to maintain the child.

Treitel agreed with Denning that performance of a duty imposed by the law can be consideration for a promise. He argues that it is public policy which accounts for the refusal of the law in certain circumstances to enforce promises to perform existing duties. Where there are no grounds of public policy involved, then a promise given in consideration of a public duty can be enforced.

He cites:

- promises to pay rewards for information leading to the arrest of a felon. See *Sykes v DPP* [1961];

Ward v Byham (above).

In most cases, it would make no difference whether the court proceeded on the basis that the matter was one of public policy or a lack of consideration. But the former ground does allow a greater degree of flexibility.

PERFORMING AN EXISTING CONTRACTUAL DUTY

Where the duty is owed to the other party, this cannot be consideration for:

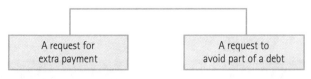

| A request for extra payment | A request to avoid part of a debt |

A request for extra payment

▶ STILK v MYRICK [1809]

Facts

The captain promised the rest of the crew extra wages if they would sail the ship back home after two sailors had deserted.

Held

The crew were unable to enforce the promise, as they were already bound by their contract to meet the normal emergencies of the voyage and were doing no more than their original contractual duty in working the ship home.

■ Where the promisor, however, performs more than he had originally promised, then there can be consideration.

▶ HARTLEY v PONSONBY [1857]

Facts

Nearly half the crew deserted the voyage. This discharged the contracts of the remaining sailors as it was dangerous to sail the ship home with only half the crew.

Held

The sailors were free to make a new bargain, so the captain's promise to pay them additional wages was enforceable.

Exceptions to the rule in *Stilk v Myrick*:

Factual advantages obtained by the promisor

An exception to the rule that performance of an existing contractual obligation owed to the promisor will not amount to consideration will occur where a party can be seen to receive an extra benefit from the other party's agreement to carry out his existing obligations.

❯ WILLIAMS v ROFFEY BROS [1991]

Facts

The defendants (the main contractors) were refurbishing a block of flats. They sub-contracted the carpentry work to the plaintiff. The plaintiff ran into financial difficulties, whereupon the defendants agreed to pay the plaintiff an additional sum if they completed the work on time.

Held

Where a party to an existing contract later agrees to pay an 'extra bonus' in order that the other party performs his obligations under the original contract, then the new agreement is binding if the party agreeing to pay the bonus has thereby obtained some new practical advantage or avoided a disadvantage. In this particular case, the advantage was the avoidance of a penalty clause and the expense of finding new carpenters, among other factors.

▦ Note – *Stilk v Myrick* (above) recognises as consideration only those acts which the promisee was not under a legal obligation to perform. *Williams v Roffey Bros* (above) provides a limited exception to this rule, where the promisor obtains real practical benefit.

▦ This decision pushes to the fore the principles of economic duress as a means of distinguishing enforceable and unenforceable modifications to a contract (see Chapter 5 on economic duress). It is clear evidence that the courts are prepared to permit commercially reasonable renegotiation of an existing contract which benefits both parties and not prevent this by taking an excessively technical view of consideration. However, factual benefit can constitute consideration only where the new promise has not been extorted by fraud or duress. There is considerable controversy as to whether *Williams v Roffey Bros* and *Stilk v Myrick* can be reconciled.

Duties owed to third party

Where a duty is owed to a third party, its performance can also be consideration for a promise by another. It is clear that the third party is getting something more than he is entitled to.

- In *Shadwell v Shadwell* [1860], an uncle promised to pay an annual sum to his nephew on hearing of his intended marriage. The fact of the marriage provided consideration, although the nephew was already legally contracted to marry his fiancée.

- In *Scotson v Pegg* [1861], A agreed to deliver coal to B's order. B ordered A to deliver coal to C who promised A to unload it. Held – A could enforce C's promise as A's delivery of the coal was good consideration, notwithstanding that he was already bound to do so by his contract with B.

- In *New Zealand Shipping Co v Satterthwaite & Co Ltd, The Eurymedon* [1975], it was held by the Privy Council that, where a stevedore, at the request of the consignee of certain goods, removed the goods from a ship, this was consideration for the promise by the consignee to give the stevedore the benefit of an exclusion clause, although the stevedore in removing the goods was only performing contractual duties he owed to the carrier.

A request to avoid part of a debt

Basic rule: payment of a smaller sum will not discharge the duty to pay a higher sum

If a creditor is owed £100 and agrees to accept £90 in full settlement, he can later insist on the remaining £10 being paid as there is no consideration for his promise to waive the £10 (the rule in *Pinnel's Case* [1602]).

▨ This rule was confirmed by the HOL in *Foakes v Beer* [1884].

▶ FOAKES v BEER [1884]

Facts

Dr Foakes was indebted to Mrs Beer on a judgment sum of £2,090. It was agreed by Mrs Beer that, if Foakes paid her £500 in cash and the balance of £1,590 in instalments, she would not take 'any proceedings whatsoever' on the judgment. Foakes paid the money exactly as requested, but Mrs Beer then proceeded to claim an additional £360 as interest on the judgment debt. Foakes refused and, when sued, pleaded that his duty to pay interest had been discharged by the promise not to sue.

Held

HOL deferred as to whether, on its true construction, the agreement merely gave Foakes time to pay or was intended to cover interest as well. But they held, even on the latter construction, there was no consideration for the promise and that Foakes was still bound to pay the additional sum.

There are situations, however, where payment of a smaller sum will discharge the liability for the higher sum:

▨ where the promise to accept a smaller sum in full settlement is made by deed, or in return for consideration;

▨ where the original claim was not for a fixed sum or the amount is disputed in good faith;

▨ where the debtor does something different, for example, where payment is made, at the creditor's request,

● at an earlier time;

● at a different place;

● by a different method (it was held in *D & C Builders Ltd v Rees* [1966] that payment by cheque is not payment by a different method);

▨ where payment is accompanied by an additional benefit;

▨ in a composition agreement with creditors;

▨ where payment is made by a third party (see *Hirachand Punachand v Temple* [1911]).

It has been argued that to allow the creditor to sue for the remaining debt would be a fraud on the third parties in the last two cases above.

Note – the doctrine of promissory estoppel, under certain circumstances, may allow payment of a smaller sum to discharge liability for the larger sum.

In *Re Selectmove* [1995], the COA refused to extend the principle laid down in *Williams v Roffey Bros* to part payment of a debt. The company had offered to pay its arrears by instalments to the Inland Revenue who said that they would let them know if this was acceptable. They heard nothing further, but paid some instalments and then received a threat of being wound up if the full arrears were not paid immediately. The court was not prepared to allow *Williams v Roffey Bros* to overturn the rule in *Foakes v Beer*.

PROMISSORY ESTOPPEL

If a promise, intended to be binding, and intended to be acted upon, is acted upon, then the court will not allow the promisor to go back on his promise

There are problems with regard to:

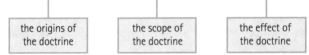

| the origins of the doctrine | the scope of the doctrine | the effect of the doctrine |

ORIGINS

- It was introduced (*obiter*) by Lord Denning in the *Central London Property Trust Ltd v High Trees House Ltd* [1947] where owners of a block of flats had promised to accept reduced rents in 1939. There was no consideration for their promise, but Lord Denning nevertheless stated that he would estop them from recovering any arrears. He based his statement on the decision in *Hughes v Metropolitan Railway* [1877].

- It would, however, seem to conflict with the HOL decision in *Jorden v Money* [1854] where it was stated that estoppel applied only to statements of fact and not to promises, and also with the decision in *Foakes v Beer* [1884] where the HOL confirmed that payment of a smaller sum will not discharge the liability for a larger sum.

SCOPE

> The exact scope of the doctrine is a matter of debate; but certain requirements must be met

- Estoppel only applies to the modification or discharge of an existing contractual obligation. It cannot create a new contract. See *Combe v Combe* [1951] above. (However, it was used to create a new right of action in the Australian case of *Waltons v Maher* [1988].)

- It can be used only as a 'shield and not a sword'.

- The promise not to enforce rights must be clear and unequivocal. In *The Scaptrade* [1983], the mere fact of not having enforced one's full rights in the past was not sufficient.

- It must be inequitable for the promisor to go back on his promise. In *D & C Builders v Rees* [1966], Mrs Rees had forced the builders to accept her cheque by inequitable means and so could not rely on promissory estoppel.

- The promisee must have acted in reliance on the promise, although not necessarily to his detriment (*Alan & Co Ltd v El-Nasr Export and Import Co* [1972]).

EFFECT OF THE DOCTRINE

It is not clear whether the doctrine extinguishes rights, or merely suspends them

This question is particulary important in single payment contracts.

▨ In *Tool Metal Manufacturing Co v Tungsten Electric Co* [1955], the owner of a patent promised to suspend periodic payments during the war. It was held by the COA that the promise was binding for the duration of the war but the owners could, on giving reasonable notice at the end of the war, revert to their original legal entitlements.

▨ In *Ajayi v Briscoe* [1964], the Privy Council stated that the promisor could resile from his promise on giving reasonable notice which allowed the promisee a reasonable opportunity of resuming his position, but that the promise would become final if the promisee could not resume his former position.

On one interpretation, these cases show that, as regards existing or past obligations, it is extinctive; but, as regards future obligations, it is suspensory.

On another interpretation, the correct approach is to look at the nature of the promise. If it was intended to be permanent, then the promisee's liability will be extinguished.

Lord Denning consistently asserted that promissory estoppel can extinguish debts. However, this view is contrary to *Foakes v Beer*.

The view that promissory estoppel is suspensory only would reconcile it with the decisions in *Jorden v Money*, *Foakes v Beer* and *Pinnel's Case* but it would deprive it of most of its usefulness.

INTENTION TO BE LEGALLY BOUND

Commercial and business agreements

Social and domestic agreements

In commercial and business agreements, there is a presumption that the parties intend to create legal relations

This presumption may be rebutted but the onus of proof is on the party seeking to exclude legal relations.

▶ ESSO PETROLEUM CO LTD v COMMISSIONERS OF CUSTOMS AND EXCISE [1976]

Facts

Esso promised to give one world cup coin with every four gallons of petrol sold. The question for the court was whether or not there was a contractual right to the coins.

Held

A majority of the HOL believed that the presumption in favour of legal relations had not been rebutted, as the transaction took place in a setting of business relations. The coins were of very little value, but were attractive to customers, thus helping the garage to derive a commercial benefit from the promotion.

EXAMPLES OF REBUTTALS

▨ 'This arrangement is not entered into . . . as a formal or legal agreement, and shall not be subject to legal jurisdiction in the law courts' (*Rose and Frank v Crompton Bros* [1925]).

▨ Agreement to be binding 'in honour only' (*Jones v Vernon Pools* [1939]).

▨ Letters of comfort, for example, statements to encourage lending to an associated company. It was held in *Kleinwort Benson Ltd v Malaysia Mining Corpn* [1989] that the defendant's statement that 'it is our policy to ensure that the business is at all times in a position to meet its liabilities to you' was a statement of present fact and not a promise for the future. As such, it was not intended to create legal relations.

▨ Collective agreements are declared not to be legally binding by the Trade

Unions and Labour Relations (Consolidation) Act 1992 unless expressly stated in writing to be so.

> In social and domestic agreements, there is a presumption against legal relations

This can be rebutted by evidence to the contrary, for example:

- Agreements between husband and wife. In *Balfour v Balfour* [1919], the court refused to enforce a promise by the husband to give his wife £50 per month whilst he was working abroad. However, the court will enforce a clear agreement where the parties are separating or separated (*Merritt v Merritt* [1970]).

- Agreements between members of a family.

▶ JONES v PADAVATTON [1969]

Facts

Mrs Jones offered a monthly allowance to her daughter if she would come to England to read for the Bar. Her daughter agreed but was not very successful. Mrs Jones stopped paying the monthly allowance but allowed her daughter to live in her house and receive the rents from other tenants. Mrs Jones later sued for possession. The daughter counterclaimed for breach of the agreement to pay the monthly allowance and/or for accommodation.

Held

(a) the first agreement may have been made with the intention of creating legal relations, but was for a reasonable time and would in any case have lapsed;

(b) the second agreement was a family arrangement without an intention to create legal relations. It was very vague and uncertain.

■ An intention to be legally bound may be inferred where:

● one party has acted to his detriment on the agreement (*Parker v Clark* [1960]); or

● a business arrangement is involved (*Snelling v Snelling* [1973]); or

● there is mutuality (*Simpkins v Pays* [1955]).

But, in all such cases, the terms of the agreement must be clear.

You should now be confident that you would be able to tick all of the boxes on the checklist at the beginning of this chapter. To check your knowledge of Consideration why not visit the companion website and take the Multiple Choice Question test. Check your understanding of the terms and vocabulary used in this chapter with the flashcard glossary.

Contents of a contract

3

Once a contract has been formed, it is necessary to define the scope of the obligations which each party incurs.

(Incorporation of terms is covered in Chapter 4.)

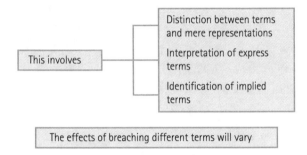

This involves

Distinction between terms and mere representations

Interpretation of express terms

Identification of implied terms

The effects of breaching different terms will vary

THE DISTINCTION BETWEEN TERMS AND MERE REPRESENTATIONS

Is a statement part of the contract? Statements made during negotiations leading to a contract may be either:

▨ Terms:

Statements which form the express terms of the contract. As such they constitute promises as to the present truth of the statement, or as to future action. If such a promise is broken (for example, because the statement is untrue) this will be a breach of contract; or

▨ Mere representations:

Statements that do not form part of the contract, but which helped to induce the contract. If these are untrue, they are 'misrepresentations'.

(Misrepresentation is covered in Chapter 5.)

Now that damages can be awarded for negligent misrepresentation, the distinction has lost much of its former significance, but there are still some important consequences.

> Whether a statement has become a term of the contract depends on the intention of the parties

In trying to ascertain such intention, the court may take into account the following factors.

THE IMPORTANCE OF THE STATEMENT TO THE PARTIES

▪ In *Bannerman v White* [1861], the buyer stated 'if sulphur has been used, I do not want to know the price'. Held – it was a term of the contract that sulphur was not used. Similarly, in *Couchman v Hill* [1947], the buyer asked if the cow was in calf, stating that if she was, he would not bid. The auctioneer's reply that she was not in calf was held to be a term overriding the printed conditions which excluded any warranty.

THE RESPECTIVE KNOWLEDGE OF THE PARTIES

Where a statement is made by a person with expert knowledge or skill relevant to the contract matter, the courts are likely to find that the statement is a term.

▶ OSCAR CHESS LTD v WILLIAMS [1957]

Facts

The defendant (a private individual) wished to trade his old car in and purchase a new one. The part exchange price depended on the age of the car. The defendant, having taken his information from the registration book, told the car dealer that it was a 1948 model.

Held

A statement by a member of the public (a non-expert) to a garage (an expert) with regard to the age of a car was a mere representation not a term.

▪ On the other hand,

> ▶ DICK BENTLEY PRODUCTIONS LTD v HAROLD SMITH
> (MOTORS) LTD [1965]
>
> Facts
>
> The defendant (a car dealer) informed the plaintiff that a car he was
> selling had had its gearbox and engine replaced, and had accumu-
> lated only 20,000 miles since the replacements. It later transpired
> that the car had done almost 100,000 since the replacements.
>
> Held
>
> The statement made by a garage (an expert) to a member of the
> public (a non-expert) concerning the mileage of a car was held to be
> a term.

THE MANNER OF THE STATEMENT

▪ For example, if it suggests verification (*Ecay v Godfrey* [1947]), it is unlikely
to be a term. If it discourages verification, 'If there was anything wrong with
the horse, I would tell you' (*Schawel v Reade* [1913]), it is more likely to be
a term.

WHERE A CONTRACT HAS BEEN REDUCED TO WRITING

The terms will normally be the statements incorporated into the written
contract (*Routledge v McKay* [1954]).

▪ But, a contract may be partly oral and partly written (see *Couchman v
Hill* [1947] above). In *Evans & Sons Ltd v Andrea Merzario Ltd* [1976], an
oral assurance that machinery would be stowed under, not on, the deck was
held to be a term of a contract, although it was not incorporated into the
written terms. The court held that the contract was partly oral and partly
written, and, in such hybrid circumstances, the court was entitled to look at
all the circumstances.

▪ Note – the discovery of a collateral contract may overcome the difficulties
of oral warranties in written contracts.

> ❱ CITY OF WESTMINSTER PROPERTIES v MUDD [1959]

Facts

A tenant signed a lease containing a covenant to use the premises for business purposes only. He was induced to sign by a statement that this clause did not apply to him and that he could continue to sleep on the premises.

Held

The tenant's signing of the contract was consideration for this promise, thus creating a collateral contract.

In *Evans & Son Ltd v Andrea Merzario Ltd* [1976], Lord Denning considered the oral statement to be a collateral contract. In *Esso Petroleum Co v Mardon* [1976], the court held that the statement by a representative of Esso with regard to the throughput of a petrol station was covered by an implied collateral warranty that the statement had been made with due care and skill.

▓ The use of a collateral contract will not be possible, however, if the main contract contains an appropriately worded 'entire agreement' clause (*The Inntrepreneur Pub Co (GL) v East Crown Ltd* [2000]).

IDENTIFICATION OF EXPRESS TERMS

▓ See incorporation of terms in Chapter 4.

INTERPRETATION OF EXPRESS TERMS OF A CONTRACT

Oral contracts

The contents are a matter of evidence for the judge. The interpretation will be undertaken by applying an objective test: what would a reasonable person have understood the words to mean? (*Thake v Maurice* [1986].)

'The question is what a reasonable person . . . would have understood the parties to have meant by the use of specific language. The answer to that question is to be gathered from the text under consideration and its relevant contextual scene' (*Sirius International Insurance Co (Publ) v FAI General Insurance Ltd* [2005]).

Five principles of interpretation were outlined by Lord Hoffmann in *Investors Compensation Scheme Ltd v West Bromwich Building Society* [1998]:

1   Need to ascertain the meaning the document would convey to a reasonable person with all the information the parties would reasonably have had available to them.
2   The background of the contract aids interpretation.
3   Previous negotiations of the parties and declarations of subjective intent are inadmissable as evidence of the meaning of a contract.
4   The meaning of a term is not simply that conveyed by literal interpretation of its words.
5   Words should usually be given their ordinary meaning, unless there is evidence of contrary intention.

Written contracts

If a contract is reduced to writing, then, under the 'parol evidence' rule, oral or other evidence extrinsic to the document is not normally admissible to 'add to, vary, or contradict' (*Jacobs v Batavia and General Plantations Trust* [1924]) the terms of the written agreement.

Exceptions to the parol evidence rule

■ to show that the contract is not legally binding, for example, because of mistake;

■ to show that the contract is subject to a 'condition precedent'. In *Pym v Campbell* [1856], oral evidence was admitted to show that a contract was not to come into operation unless a patent was approved by a third party;

■ to establish a custom or trade usage (*Hutton v Warren* [1836], see below);

■ to rebut the presumption that the written contract contains the entire agreement. See *Couchman v Hill* [1947] and *Evans v Andrea Merzario* (above);

■ a contract may be contained in more than one document (*Jacobs v Batavia Plantation Trust Ltd* [1924]);

■ to establish a collateral contract (*City of Westminster Properties Ltd v Mudd* [1959] ; *Evans & Son Ltd v Andrea Merzario Ltd* (above)).

The Law Commission recommended in 1976 that the 'parol evidence' rule be abolished. However, in view of the wide exceptions to the rule, it recommended in 1986 that no action need be taken.

IDENTIFICATION OF IMPLIED TERMS

In addition to the terms which the parties have expressly agreed, a court may be prepared to hold that other terms must be implied into the contract. Such terms may be implied by:

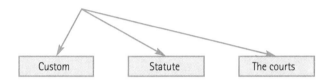

| Custom | Statute | The courts |

CUSTOM

A contract may be deemed to incorporate any relevant custom of the market, trade or locality in which the contract is made.

In *Hutton v Warren* [1836], a tenant established a right to fair allowance for improvements to the land through a local custom.

STATUTE

Parliament, as a matter of public policy, has in various instances seen fit to imply terms into contracts, for example the Sale of Goods Act 1979, which implies the following terms into contracts for the sale of goods.

Terms implied into all sales:

- that the seller has the right to sell the goods;

- that goods sold by description correspond with the description.

Terms implied only into sales by way of business:

- that the goods are of satisfactory quality. Goods are of a satisfactory quality if they meet the standard that a reasonable person would regard as satisfactory, taking account of any description of the goods, the price, if relevant, and all other relevant circumstances. In particular, it will be necessary to consider their:

● fitness for all purposes for which goods of that kind are commonly supplied;

● appearance and finish;

● freedom from minor defects;

● safety; and

● durability.

(This term does not apply to matters specifically drawn to the buyer's attention before the contract is made or, where the buyer examines the goods, defects which that examination should have revealed.)

▨ that the goods are fit for any special purpose made known to the seller;

▨ that goods sold by sample correspond with the sample.

The Supply of Goods and Services Act 1982 implies similar terms into contracts of hire, contracts for work and materials, and other contracts not covered by the Sale of Goods Act.

▨ In contracts of service, there is an implied term that the service will be carried out with reasonable care and skill, within a reasonable time and for a reasonable price.

In *Wilson v Best* [1993], it was held that the duty of a travel agent under this provision extended to checking that the local safety regulations had been complied with. It did not require them to ensure that they complied with UK regulations.

THE COURTS

| Terms implied in fact | Terms implied in law |

Terms implied in fact

When interpreting terms implied in fact, the court seeks to give effect to the unexpressed intention of the parties. There are two tests. A term may be implied because:

- It is necessary to give business efficacy to the contract. In *The Moorcock* [1889], a term was implied that the riverbed was in a condition that would not damage a ship unloading at the jetty.

- It satisfies the 'officious bystander' test, that is, if a bystander suggested a term, the parties would respond with a common 'of course'. In *Spring v NASDS* [1956], the union tried to imply the 'Bridlington Agreement'. The court refused on the basis that if an 'officious bystander had suggested this, the plaintiff would have replied "What's that?" '.

The *Moorcock* doctrine is used in order to make the contract workable, or where it was so obvious that the parties must have intended it to apply to the agreement. It will not be used merely because it was reasonable or because it would improve the contract.

It was suggested in *Shell UK Ltd v Lostock Garages Ltd* [1977] that the courts will be reluctant to imply a term where the parties have entered into a detailed and carefully drafted written agreement.

Terms implied in law

- When terms are implied in law, they are implied into all contracts of a particular kind. Here, the court is not trying to put into effect the parties' intention, but is imposing an obligation on one party, often as a matter of public policy. For example, the court implies into all contracts of employment a term that the employee will carry out his work with reasonable care and skill and will indemnify his employer against any loss caused by his negligence (*Lister v Romford Ice Cold Storage Co* [1957]).

- In these cases, the implication is not based on the presumed intention of the parties, but on the court's perception of the nature of the relationship between the parties, and whether such an implied term was reasonable.

- In *Liverpool CC v Irwin* [1977], the tenants of a block of council flats failed to persuade the court to imply a term that the council should be responsible for the common parts of the building on the *Moorcock* or 'officious bystander' test, but succeeded on the basis of the *Lister* test, that is, the term should be implied in law in that the agreement was incomplete, it involved the relationship of landlord and tenant and it would be reasonable to expect the landlord to be responsible for the common parts of the building.

CLASSIFICATION OF TERMS

| Conditions | Warranties | Innominate terms |

There is a very important distinction between those terms of a contract which entitle an innocent party to terminate (rescind, or treat as discharged) a contract in the event of a breach, and those which merely enable a person to claim damages.

Traditionally, a distinction has been made in English law between the following.

CONDITIONS

> Statements of fact or promises which form the essential terms of the contract. If the statement is not true, or the promise is not fulfilled, the injured party may terminate (or treat as discharged) the contract and claim damages

▪ The Sale of Goods Act 1979 designates certain implied terms, for example, re satisfactory quality, as conditions – the breach of which entitles the buyer to terminate (or treat as discharged) the contract.

▶ POUSSARD v SPIERS AND POND [1876]

Facts

An actress who had contracted to perform the lead role in an operetta for a full season failed to take up a role in an opera, due to illness, until a week after the season had started.

Held

Her promise to perform as from the first performance was fundamental to the contract, thus constituting a condition, the breach of which entitled the management to treat the contract as discharged.

WARRANTIES

Contractual terms concerning the less important or subsidiary statements of facts or promises. If a warranty is broken, this does not entitle the other party to terminate (or treat as discharged) the contract, it merely entitles him to sue for damages

- The Sale of Goods Act 1979 designates certain terms as warranties, breach of which does not allow the buyer to treat the contract as discharged, but merely to sue for damages, for example, the right to quiet enjoyment.

▶ BETTINI v GYE [1876]

Breach of warranty in a contract will not entitle the other party to terminate the contract, it merely enables the wronged party to sue for damages.

Facts

A singer was engaged to sing for a whole season and to arrive six days in advance to take part in rehearsals. He arrived only three days in advance.

Held

The rehearsal clause was a warranty, as it was subsidiary to the main clause.

The management were therefore not entitled to treat the contract as discharged. They should have kept to the original contract and sought damages for the three days' delay.

INNOMINATE OR INTERMEDIATE TERMS

In *Hong Kong Fir Shipping Co v Kawasaki Kisen Kaisha* [1962], it was suggested by the COA that it was not enough to classify terms into conditions and warranties. Regard should also be had to the character and nature of the breach which has occurred.

❱ HONG KONG FIR SHIPPING CO v KAWASAKI KISEN KAISHA [1962]

Facts

The defendants chartered the vessel *Hong Kong Fir* to the plaintiffs for 24 months; the charter party provided that the ship was 'fitted in every way for ordinary cargo service'. The vessel spent less than nine weeks of the first seven months at sea because of breakdowns and the consequent repairs which were necessary.

Held

The term was neither a condition nor a warranty, and in determining whether the defendants could terminate the contract, it was necessary to look at the consequences of the breach, to see if it deprived the innocent party of substantially the whole benefit he should have received under the contract.

On the facts, this was not the case because the charter party still had a substantial time to run.

After the *Hong Kong Fir* case in 1962, there was some confusion as to whether the breach-based test which applied to innominate terms had replaced the term-based test which relied on the distinction between conditions and warranties, or merely added to it an alternative in certain circumstances.

▶ THE MIHALIS ANGELOS [1970]

Facts

COA reverted to the term-based test. The owners of a vessel stated that the vessel was 'expected ready to load' on or about 1 July. It was discovered that this was not so.

Held

The term was a condition – the charterers could treat the contract as discharged.

In 1976, two cases were decided on the breach-based principle.

▶ CEHAVE v BREMER HANDELSGESELLSCHAFT MBH, THE HANSA NORD [1976]

Facts

The seller had sold a cargo of citrus pellets with a term in the contract that the shipment be made in good condition. The buyer rejected the cargo on the basis that this term had been broken. The defect, however, was not serious.

Held

Although the Sale of Goods Act 1979 had classified some terms as conditions and warranties, it did not follow that all the terms had to be so classified. Accordingly, the court could consider the effect of the breach; since this was not serious, the buyer had not been entitled to reject.

▶ REARDON SMITH v HANSEN TANGEN [1976]

Facts

An oil tanker was described as 'Osaka No 354', where in fact it was 'Oshima No 004', but was otherwise exactly as specified. Because the market for oil tankers had collapsed, the charterers sought to argue that the number was a condition which would enable them to repudiate the contract.

Held

HOL rejected this argument. The statement was an innominate term, not a condition; since the effect of the breach was trivial, it did not justify termination of the contract.

Note – the time for determining whether a clause was a condition or an innominate term is at the time of contracting, not after the breach.

Traditionally, a term is a condition if it has been established as such:

- By statute – for example, the Sale of Goods Act 1979.

- By precedent after a judicial decision. In *The Mihalis Angelos* [1970], the COA held that the 'expected readiness' clause in a charter party is a condition.

- By the intention of the parties. The court must ascertain the intention of the parties. If the wording clearly indicates that the parties intended that breach of a particular term should give rise to a right to rescind, that term will be regarded as a condition.

▶ LOMBARD NORTH CENTRAL v BUTTERWORTH [1987]

Facts

COA held that contracting parties can provide expressly in the contract that 'specific breaches could terminate the contract'. In this case, the contract included an express clause that the time for payment of instalments was 'of the essence of the contract'. An accountant had contracted to hire a computer for five years, agreeing to make an initial payment and 19 quarterly rental payments. He was late in paying some instalments, and the owners terminated the agreement, recovered possession of the computer, and claimed damages for the arrears and loss of future instalments.

Held

The claim succeeded because the contract specifically stated that the time of payment of each instalment was to be of the essence of the contract.

Note: the mere use of the word 'condition' is not conclusive.

In *Schuler v Wickman Tool Sales Ltd* [1974], the HOL held that breach of a 'condition' that a distributor should visit six customers every week could not have been intended to allow rescission. The word 'condition' had not been used in this particular sense. There was in the contract a separate clause which indicated when and how the contract could be terminated.

▨ By the court – deciding according to the subject matter of the contract (see *Poussard v Spiers* [1876] and *Bettini v Gye* [1876] above).

If a term is not a condition, then the 'wait and see' technique can be used to decide whether the gravity of the breach is such that it deprived the innocent party of substantially the whole benefit of the contract. If so, the innocent party can terminate the contract (innominate or intermediate term)

CERTAINTY AND FLEXIBILITY

CERTAINTY

▨ The term-based test is alleged to have the advantage of predictability and certainty. It is important for the parties to know their legal rights and liabilities as regards the availability of termination. The character of all terms is ascertainable at the moment the contract is concluded. If the term is a condition, then the parties will know that its breach allows the other party to terminate. However, there may still be uncertainty where the parties have to await the court's classification of the term.

▨ The advantage of certainty is, however, balanced by the fact that it is possible to terminate a contract for what may be a minor breach, eg *Arcos Ltd v E. A. Ronaasen* [1933].

FLEXIBILITY

▧ The breach-based test arguably brings flexibility to the law. Instead of saying that the innocent party can, in the case of a condition, always terminate or, in the case of a warranty, never terminate, innominate terms allow the courts to permit termination where the circumstances justify it and the consequences are sufficiently serious.

▧ It is, however, more difficult for the innocent party to know when he has the right to terminate, or for the party in breach to realise in advance the consequence of his action.

Note – the distinction between the different types of contract terms remains of considerable importance.

You should now be confident that you would be able to tick all of the boxes on the checklist at the beginning of this chapter. To check your knowledge of Contents of a contract why not visit the companion website and take the Multiple Choice Question test. Check your understanding of the terms and vocabulary used in this chapter with the flashcard glossary.

4

Exemption
(exclusion or limitation)
clauses

Incorporation	☐
Unfair Contract Terms Act (UCTA) 1977	☐
Reasonableness test	☐
Unfair Terms in Consumer Contracts Regulations 1999	☐
Unfairness	☐

> A clause which purports to exclude, wholly or in part, liability for a breach of contract or a tort

A total exclusion is referred to as an exclusion clause; a partial exclusion is known as a limitation clause.

Exemption clauses are most commonly found in standard form contracts.

To be valid, an exemption clause must satisfy the tests set by the:

| Common law | Unfair Contract Terms Act (UCTA) 1977 | Regulations on Unfair Terms in Consumer Contracts 1999 |

COMMON LAW REQUIREMENTS

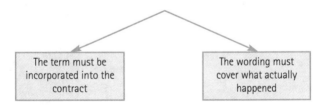

| The term must be incorporated into the contract | The wording must cover what actually happened |

INCORPORATION

■ This requirement applies to all terms, but has been interpreted strictly in the case of exemption clauses. A term may be incorporated into a contract by being:

Contained in a signed document

In *L'Éstrange v Graucob Ltd* [1934], the plaintiff had signed a contract of sale without reading it. Held – she was bound by the terms which contained an exemption clause.

Exceptions

Where the offeree has been induced to sign as a result of misrepresentation.

> ### ▶ CURTIS v CHEMICAL CLEANING CO [1951]
>
> Facts
>
> The plaintiff signed a 'receipt' when she took a dress to be cleaned, on being told that it was to protect the cleaners in case of damage to the sequins. In fact, the clause excluded liability for all damage.
>
> Held
>
> The cleaners were not protected for damage to the dress; the extent of the clause had been misrepresented and therefore the cleaners could not rely on it.

Contained in an unsigned document (ticket cases)

- It must be clear that this is a contractual document.

> ### ▶ CHAPELTON v BARRY UDC [1940]
>
> Facts
>
> On hiring a deck chair, the plaintiff was given a ticket with only a large black 3d on the face of the ticket, and exclusion clauses on the back.
>
> Held
>
> The defendants could not rely on the exclusion clauses as it was not apparent on the face of it that the ticket was a contractual document, rather than just a receipt.

- Reasonable notice of the term must be given. Whether notice is reasonable depends on the facts of the case and the nature of the clause. See below:

▶ PARKER v SOUTH EASTERN RAILWAY CO [1877]

Facts

The plaintiff left some luggage in the cloakroom at a station. He received a ticket which stated on the face 'see back', which contained a clause limiting the liability of the railway company for any loss, for luggage exceeding £10 in value. The luggage was stolen (and was worth more than £10).

Held

As long as the railway company had given reasonable notice of the exemption clause's existence, it did not matter that the plaintiff had not read the clause.

▶ THOMPSON v LONDON MIDLAND AND SCOTTISH RAILWAY [1930]

Facts

The plaintiff, who was illiterate, was injured as a result of alleged negligence by the railway company. The ticket indicated that the conditions of the contract could be seen at the station master's office, or on the timetable. The exemption clause was in clause 552 of the timetable which cost sixpence – the ticket itself only cost two and sixpence.

Held

The clause had been incorporated into the contract and reasonable notice had been given.

● The test is objective, and it is irrelevant that the party affected by the exemption clause is blind or illiterate, or otherwise unable to understand it (*Thompson v London Midland and Scottish Railway*, above).

● But, in *Geir v Kujawa* [1970], a notice in English was stuck on the windscreen of a car stating that passengers travelled at their own risk. A German passenger who was known to speak no English was held not to be bound by the clause as reasonable care had not been taken to bring it to his attention. It is arguably difficult to reconcile this case with *Thompson v London Midland and Scottish Railway*.

▨ Attention must be drawn to any unusual clause.

● In *Thornton v Shoe Lane Parking* [1971], it was stated that a person who drives his car into a car park might expect to find in his contract a clause excluding liability for loss or damage to the car; but special notice should have been given of a clause purporting to exclude liability for personal injury.

● In *Interfoto Picture Library v Stiletto Visual Programmes* [1989], the COA confirmed that onerous conditions required special measures to bring them to the attention of the defendant. The clause in that case was not an exemption clause, but a clause imposing charges 10 times higher than normal. The COA stated that the more unusual the clause, the greater the notice required.

▨ Notice of the term must be communicated to the other party before, or at the time that, the contract is entered into.

● In *Thornton v Shoe Lane Parking Ltd* [1971], the plaintiff made his contract with the car company when he inserted a coin in the ticket machine. The ticket was issued afterwards, and in any case referred to conditions displayed inside the car park which he could see only after entry. Notice therefore came too late.

▨ The rules of offer and acceptance, and the distinctions between offers and invitations to treat, must be consulted in order to ascertain when the contract was made. Problems with regard to incorporation can arise in a 'Battle of the Forms' scenario. See *Butler Machine Tool Ltd v Ex-Cell-O Corpn* (Chapter 1).

NOTICE BY DISPLAY

Notices exhibited in premises seeking to exclude liability for loss or damage are common, for example, 'car parked at owner's risk' and must be seen before, or at the time of, entry into contract. See below:

▶ OLLEY v MARLBOROUGH COURT HOTEL [1949]

Facts

Mr and Mrs Olley saw a notice on the hotel bedroom wall which stated 'the proprietors will not hold themselves responsible for articles lost or stolen, unless handed to the manageress for safe keeping'. Mrs Olley sought compensation from the hotel when her fur coat was stolen. The proprietors sought to rely on the exclusion clause.

Held

The contract had been entered into on registration before the Olleys had the opportunity to read the notice on the bedroom door. The clause was therefore not incorporated into the contract and could not protect the proprietors.

NOTICE BY A 'COURSE OF DEALING'

▨ If there has been a course of dealing between the parties, the usual terms may be incorporated into the contract although not specifically drawn to the attention of the parties each time a contract is made. See below:

▶ SPURLING v BRADSHAW [1956]

Facts

Bradshaw deposited some orange juice in Spurling's warehouse. The contractual document excluding liability for loss or damage was not sent to Bradshaw until several days after the contract.

Held

The exclusion clauses were valid, as the parties had always done business with each other on this basis.

▨ Note – the transactions must be sufficiently numerous to constitute a course of dealing. The established course of dealing must be consistent, and it must not have been deviated from on the occasion in question.

In *Hollier v Rambler Motors* [1972], the COA held that bringing a car to be serviced or repaired at a garage on three or four occasions over a period of five years did not establish a course of dealing.

NOTICE THROUGH PATENT KNOWLEDGE

▶ BRITISH CRANE HIRE CORPN v IPSWICH PLANT HIRE [1975]

Facts
The owner of a crane hired it out to a contractor who was engaged in the same business.

Held
The hirer was bound by the owner's usual terms though they were not actually communicated at the time of the contract. They were, however, based on a model supplied by a trade association, to which both parties belonged. It was stated that they were reasonable, and were well known in the trade.

ORAL CONTRACTS

▨ Whether a clause has been incorporated into an oral contract is a matter of evidence for the court (*McCutcheon v MacBrayne* [1964]).

ON A PROPER CONSTRUCTION, THE CLAUSE COVERS THE LOSS IN QUESTION

▨ An exclusion clause is interpreted *contra proferentem*; any ambiguity in the clause will be interpreted against the party seeking to rely on it:

● in *Houghton v Trafalgar Insurance Co Ltd* [1954], it was held that the word 'load' could not refer to people;

● in *Andrews Bros v Singer & Co Ltd* [1934], an exclusion referring to implied terms was not allowed to cover a term that the car was new, as this was an express term.

It was, however, suggested by the HOL in *Photo Production Ltd v Securicor Ltd* [1980] that any need for a strained and distorted interpretation of contracts in order to control the effect of exemption clauses had been reduced by UCTA.

- Especially clear words must be used in order to exclude liability for negligence, for example, the use of the word 'negligence', or the phrase 'howsoever caused' (*Smith v South Wales Switchgear Ltd* [1978]).

  But, if these words are not used, provided the wording is wide enough to cover negligence, and there is no other liability to which they can apply, then it is assumed that they must have been intended to cover negligence (*Canada Steamship Lines v The King* [1952]).

- It was stated in *Ailsa Craig Fishing Co v Malvern Fishing Co* [1983] that limitation clauses may be interpreted less rigidly than exclusion clauses.

- Only a party to a contract can rely on an exclusion clause. (See Chapter 10.)

- Especially clear words are required when the breach is of a fundamental nature. In the past, Lord Denning and others argued that it was not possible to exclude breaches of contract which were deemed to be fundamental by any exclusion clause, however widely and clearly drafted.

However, the HOL confirmed in *Photo Production Ltd v Securicor Ltd* [1980] that the doctrine of fundamental breach was a rule of construction, not a rule of law. Liability for a fundamental breach could be excluded, if the words were sufficiently clear and precise.

The House also stated that:

- the decision in *Harbutt's Plasticine Ltd v Wayne Tank and Pump Co* [1970] was not good law. In that case, the Court of Appeal had held that as a fundamental breach brought a contract to an end there was no exclusion clause left to protect the perpetrator of the breach;

- there is no difference between a 'fundamental term' and a 'condition';

- a strained construction should not be put on words in an exclusion clause which are clearly and fairly susceptible of only one meaning;

- where the parties are bargaining on equal terms, they should be free to apportion risks as they wish;

- the courts should be wary of interfering with the settled practices of business people, as an exclusion clause often serves to identify who should insure against a particular loss.

UNFAIR CONTRACT TERMS ACT (UCTA) 1977

Note – the title is misleading.

- The Act does not cover all unfair contract terms, only exemption clauses.

- The Act covers certain tortious liability, as well as contractual liability. The following must be examined.

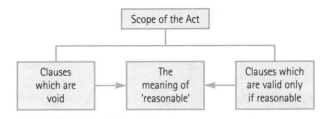

SCOPE OF THE ACT

- Section 1 – the Act applies to contracts made after 1 February 1978 which arise in the course of business. 'Business' includes a profession and the activities of any government department, and/or public or local authority.

- Section 5 – contracts specifically excluded include contracts of insurance, contracts for the transfer of land and international commercial contracts. Contracts of employment also fall outside the scope of UCTA (*Keen v Commerzbank* [2007]).

- Section 13 – the Act limits the effectiveness of clauses that exclude or restrict liability. It also covers clauses which make it difficult to enforce a contract, for example, by imposing restrictive time limits, or which exclude particular remedies.

In *Stewart Gill v Horatio Myer and Co* [1992], it was held that a clause restricting a right of set-off or counterclaim was subject to the Act. It was also held in *Smith v Bush* [1990] that it covered 'disclaimers which restrictively defined a party's obligation under a contract'. In that case, a valuation was stated to be given 'without any acceptance of liability for its accuracy'.

NEGLIGENCE

- Negligence is defined as the breach of any express or implied contractual obligation 'to take reasonable care or to exercise reasonable skill in the performance of the contract' (s 5.1).

- The Act covers contractual, tortious and statutory (for example, under the Occupiers' Liability Act 1957) negligence.

- The difference between excluding liability for negligence, and transferring liability for negligence can be seen by contrasting two cases. In *Phillips Products v Hyland Bros* [1987] the contract transferred liability for the negligence of the driver of a hired excavator to the hirer. The driver negligently damaged property belonging to the hirer. Held – the clause was an exclusion clause and was subject to UCTA.

- In *Thompson v Lohan (Plant Hire)* [1987], on the other hand, an excavator and driver were hired under the same conditions. The driver negligently killed a third party. Held – the clause transferring liability to the hirer was not an exclusion in this case as the third party was able to sue the hirer. It was merely a clause transferring liability.

MISREPRESENTATION

- The difference between excluding liability for misrepresentation, and defining the powers of an agent is seen in *Cremdean Properties v Nash* [1977] where a clause in the special conditions of sale stating that the 'particulars were believed to be correct, but their accuracy is not guaranteed' was held to be an exclusion clause.

- In *Collins v Howell Jones* [1980], however, the COA held that a statement that the 'vendor does not make or give any representation or warranty and neither the estate agent or any person in their employment has any authority to make or give a representation or warranty whatsoever in relation to the property' had the effect of defining or limiting the scope of the agent's authority.

EFFECT OF THE ACT

Clauses which are void

Exclusions of liability:

- for death or personal injury caused by negligence (s 2);

- in a manufacturer's guarantee for loss or damage caused by negligence (s 5);

- for the statutory guarantee of title in contracts for the sale of goods or hire purchase (s 6);

- for the other statutory guarantees in consumer contracts for the sale of goods or hire purchase (description, satisfactory quality, fitness for purpose) (s 6);

- for similar statutory guarantees in other consumer contracts for the supply of goods, for example, contracts of hire (s 7).

Clauses which are valid only if reasonable

Clauses excluding liability:

- for loss or damage to property caused by negligence (s 2);

- for breach of contract in a consumer or standard form contract (s 3). This includes clauses in such contracts claiming to render a substantially different performance from that reasonably expected, or to render no performance at all (s 3);

- for statutory guarantees (other than those concerning title) in inter-business contracts for the sale of goods and hire purchase (description, satisfactory quality and fitness for purpose) (s 6);

- for statutory guarantees concerning title or possession in other contracts for the supply of goods (for example, hire) (s 7);

- for other statutory guarantees (description, satisfactory quality, fitness for purpose) in other inter-business contracts for the supply of goods (s 7);

- for misrepresentation in all contracts.

Note: 'Consumer transaction' – a person is a 'consumer' where he does not make or hold himself out as making the contract in the course of business, and the other party does make the contract in the course of business. In contracts for the sale or supply of goods, the goods must also be of a type normally sold/supplied for private use where the buyer is a company, but not where the buyer is an individual.

■ A controversial interpretation of a 'consumer' was made by the COA in *R and B Customs v United Dominion Trust* [1988].

▶ R AND B CUSTOMS v UNITED DOMINION TRUST [1988]

Facts

The claimants, who operated as shipping brokers and freight forwarding agents, bought a second hand car for the business and private use of its directors.

Held

It was not bought 'in the course of a business'. Buying cars was incidental, not central to the business of the company. If it is incidental only, then the purchase would only be 'in the course of a business' if it was one made with sufficient regularity.

Note, however, that, in *Stevenson v Rogers* [1999], the COA refused to apply the *R and B Customs Brokers* approach to the question of whether a sale was in the course of a business for the purpose of s 14(12) of the Sale of Goods Act 1979.

A 'standard form contract' occurs when the parties deal on the basis of standard terms provided by one of them.

REASONABLENESS

It is for the person relying on the clause to prove that the clause is reasonable. In assessing reasonableness, the following factors should be considered:

SECTION 11 OF UCTA 1977

■ Contract terms are to be adjudged reasonable or not according to the circumstances which were, or ought reasonably to have been, known to the parties when the contract was made.

▦ Where a person seeks to restrict liability to a specified sum of money, regard should be had to the resources which he could expect to be available to him for the purpose of meeting the liability, and as to how far it was open to him to cover himself by insurance.

▦ In determining for the purpose of s 6 or s 7, whether a contract term satisfies the requirement of reasonableness, Schedule 2 of UCTA lays down certain criteria that the court may consider:

● the strength of the bargaining position of the parties relative to each other;

● whether the customer received an inducement to agree to the term and had an opportunity of entering into a similar contract with other persons but without having to accept similar terms;

● whether the customer knew, or ought reasonably to have known, of the existence and extent of the term;

● where the exclusion is conditional, whether it was reasonable to expect that compliance with that condition would be practicable;

● whether the goods were manufactured, processed, or adapted to the special order of the customer.

DECISIONS OF THE COURTS

In *Smith v Bush* [1990] and *Harris v Wyre Forest DC* [1989], the HOL dealt with two cases involving the validity of an exclusion clause protecting surveyors who had carried out valuations of a house. The HOL decided that the clauses were exclusion clauses designed to protect the surveyors against claims for negligence. Lord Griffiths declared that there were four matters which should always be considered:

▦ were the parties of equal bargaining power?;

▦ in the case of advice, would it have been reasonable to obtain advice from another source?;

▦ was the task being undertaken a difficult one, for which the protection of an exclusion clause was necessary?;

■ what would be the practical consequences for the parties of the decision on reasonableness? For example, would the defendant normally be insured? Would the claimant have to bear the cost himself?

In inter-business contracts, the practices of business people are considered.

■ In *Photo Production v Securicor* [1980], the HOL stated that the courts should be reluctant to interfere with the settled practices of businesses. They pointed out that the function of an exclusion clause was often to indicate who should insure against a particular risk.

■ In *Green v Cade Bros* [1983], it was decided that a clause requiring notice of rejection within three days of delivery of seed potatoes was unreasonable, as a defect could not have been discovered by inspection within this time, but a clause limiting damages to the contract price was upheld – as it had been negotiated by organisations representing the buyers and sellers, and 'certified' potatoes had been available for a small extra charge (that is, Sched 2 was applied).

■ However, in *George Mitchell v Finney Lock Seeds Ltd* [1983], the buyers suffered losses of £61,000, due to the supply of the wrong variety of cabbage seeds. The contract limited the liability of the seller to a refund of the price paid (£192). Held – the clause was not reasonable. Matters taken into consideration:

● the clause was inserted unilaterally – there was no negotiation;

● loss was caused by the negligence of the seller;

● the seller could have insured against his liability;

● the sellers implied that they themselves considered the clause unreasonable by accepting liability in previous cases.

■ In *Overland Shoes Ltd v Schenkers Ltd* [1998], the COA upheld a judge's ruling that a clause preventing reliance on a 'set-off' was not unreasonable, on the basis that it formed part of a set of standard trading conditions used widely in the shipping industry. They had arisen from careful negotiation, and were generally recognised in the industry as 'fair and reasonable'.

■ In *Overseas Medical Supplies Ltd v Orient Transport Services Ltd* [1999], the COA summarised the various factors that should be looked at in considering the test of reasonableness. It confirmed that the 'Guidelines' contained in Sched 2 to UCTA, although specifically intended for consumer contracts for the sale of goods, should be regarded as relevant wherever the test of reasonableness is applied. See also: *Watford Electronics Ltd v Sanderson CFL Ltd* [2001], and *Granville Oil & Chemicals Ltd v Davies Turner & Co Ltd* [2003].

In many of the cases the appeal courts have emphasised that the decision on 'reasonableness' is best made by the trial judge, and that the appeal courts should be reluctant to interfere with the conclusion arrived at at first instance.

UNFAIR TERMS IN CONSUMER CONTRACTS REGULATIONS 1999

The 1999 regulations, which implemented the EU Directive on Unfair Terms in Consumer Contracts, replaced earlier regulations made in 1994.

| Coverage | Fairness | Remedies |

COVERAGE

The regulations apply to:

> 'any term in a contract between a seller or supplier and a consumer where the term has not been individually negotiated', that is, it has been drafted in advance

This will be so, even if some other parts of the contract have not been drafted in advance.

- The regulations do not apply to contracts which relate to employment, family law, or succession rights, companies or partnerships terms included in order to comply with legislation or an international convention.

- They do, however, cover insurance policies and contracts relating to land.

- A 'business' is defined to include a trade or profession and the activities of any government department or local or public authority.

A 'consumer' means a natural person who is acting for a purpose outside his business. See *Standard Bank London Ltd v Apostolakis* [2003].

Note – they are wider than UCTA in that they cover all terms, not only exclusion clauses, for example, harsh terms concerning unauthorised overdrafts. The regulations are narrower than UCTA in that they only cover clauses in consumer contracts which have not been individually negotiated. The definition of a consumer is also narrower; cf *R and B Customs v UDT* [1988].

UNFAIRNESS

An unfair term is defined by regulation 5(1) as:

> A contractual term which has not been individually negotiated shall be regarded as unfair if, contrary to the requirements of good faith, it causes as significant imbalance in the parties' rights and obligations arising under the contract, to the detriment of the consumer.

Regard must be had to the nature of the goods and services provided, the other terms of the contract and all the circumstances relating to its conclusion. (Reg 6)

The definition of the main subject matter and the adequacy of the price or remuneration (the 'core terms' of the contract) are not subject to the test of fairness, Reg 6(2) 'Good faith' is not defined and, unlike the earlier (1994) regulations, the 1999 regulations do not spell out any relevant factors. Good faith was however considered in the case of *Director General of Fair Trading v First National Bank* (2001) wherein Lord Bingham stated that good faith was essentially a requirement of fair and open dealing.

> ▶ DIRECTOR GENERAL OF FAIR TRADING v FIRST NATIONAL BANK PLC [2000]
>
> Facts
>
> COA emphasised the need for openness and information, which will enable the consumer to make a properly informed choice about entering into the contract. In this case a clause imposing a 'surprising' requirement as to the payment of interest on a loan which had been the subject of a court order did not meet the requirement of good faith.

Held

The COA decision was reversed by the HOL (2001) on the basis that the term had been sufficiently drawn to the attention of the consumer so as not to constitute unfair surprise.

Schedule 2 of the regulations contains a long indicative list of clauses likely to be unfair. These include not only exemption clauses, but also clauses which give the seller/supplier rights without compensating rights for the consumer, for example:

▨ enabling the seller/supplier to raise the price, without giving the buyer a chance to back out if the price rise is too high;

▨ enabling the seller/supplier to cancel the agreement without penalty without also allowing the customer a similar right;

▨ automatically extending the duration of the contract, unless the customer indicates otherwise within an unreasonably brief period of time.

Note, also, that all terms (including those defining the subject matter or the price) should be expressed in plain English, and any ambiguity should be interpreted in the consumer's favour.

EFFECT OF AN UNFAIR TERM

▨ The term itself shall not be binding on the consumer, but the rest of the contract may be enforced.

▨ The Director General of Fair Trading has a duty to consider any complaint made to him that a term is unfair. He is empowered to bring proceedings for an injunction against any business using an unfair term. It was this power that was used in the first reported case on the regulations, *Director General of Fair Trading v First National Bank plc* [2000], discussed above. For the first time, a similar power to apply for such an injunction is given to certain other 'qualifying bodies', including the Data Protection Registrar, various Directors General (of gas supply, electricity supply, telecommunications, water services) and the Consumers' Association.

The Office of Fair Trading is currently investigating the fairness of bank charges levied by several high street banks. See *Office of Fair Trading v Abbey National PLC and 7 others* [2008].

In an attempt to harmonise consumer laws in EU States, the Unfair Commercial Practices Directive 2005 was passed. The Directive was implemented in the UK by the Consumer Protection from Unfair Trading Regulations 2008. The purpose of the regulations is to prevent aggressive selling methods which are unfair to consumers, such as pressure selling and unfair advertising. The regulations provide that a seller will commit an offence if he 'knowingly or recklessly engages in a commercial practice which contravenes the requirements of professional diligence' and 'the practice materially distorts or is likely to materially distort the economic behaviour of the average customer' (Reg 8).

Schedule 1 contains an extensive list of specific criminalised activities which will be deemed unfair in all circumstances.

Some of the schedules on unfair practices are:
—   falsely stating that a product will only be available for a limited time;
—   claiming to offer a competition or prize promotion without awarding the prizes;
—   describing a product as 'free' when the customer has to pay something (other than delivery);
—   making persistent and unwanted solicitations by telephone, fax or email.

You should now be confident that you would be able to tick all of the boxes on the checklist at the beginning of this chapter. To check your knowledge of Exemption (exclusion or limitation) clauses why not visit the companion website and take the Multiple Choice Question test. Check your understanding of the terms and vocabulary used in this chapter with the flashcard glossary.

5

Vitiating elements which render a contract voidable

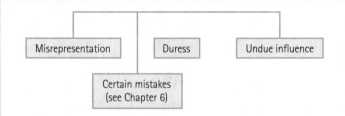

SIGNIFICANCE OF A CONTRACT BEING VOIDABLE

The innocent party may set the contract aside, if he so wishes

Thus:

▦ The innocent party may, if he wishes, affirm the contract.

▦ Where the innocent party has not performed the contract, he may refuse to perform and rely on the misrepresentation, duress or undue influence as a defence.

▦ The misled or coerced party may rescind the contract:

  ● by informing the other party; or

  ● where a fraudulent party cannot be traced, by informing the police (*Car and Universal Finance Co v Caldwell* [1965]); or

  ● by bringing legal proceedings.

▦ It was stated in *TSB v Camfield* [1995] that the right to rescind is that of the representee not the court. All the court can do is decide whether the representee has lawfully exercised the right to rescind. It is not therefore an exercise of equitable relief by the court.

RESCISSION

Restoring the parties as far as is possible to the position they were in before they entered into the contract:

▦ But, in *Cheese v Thomas* [1993], the court declared that the court must look at all the circumstances to do what was 'fair and just'. In that case, a house which had been jointly bought had to be sold afterwards at a considerable loss.

The agreement between the two parties for the purchase of the house was rescinded, but the court held that it was not necessary for the guilty party to bear the whole of the loss.

It was fair and just that the proceeds should be divided according to the parties' respective contributions.

- This contrasts with the normal situation where a property has diminished in value, and the misled party would get all his money returned (*Erlanger v New Sombrero Phosphate Co* [1878]).

- As part of this restoration, equity may order a sum of money to be paid to the misled person to indemnify him against any obligations necessarily created by the Contract.

▶ WHITTINGTON v SEALE-HAYNE [1900]

Facts

The plaintiffs, breeders of prize poultry, were induced to take a lease of the defendant's premises by his innocent misrepresentation that the premises were in a sanitary condition. Under the lease, the plaintiffs covenanted to execute all works required by any local or public authority. Owing to the insanitary conditions of the premises, the water supply was poisoned, the plaintiffs' manager and his family became very ill, and the poultry became valueless for breeding purposes or died. In addition, the local authority required the drains to be renewed. The plaintiffs sought an indemnity for all their losses.

Held

The court rescinded the lease, and held that the plaintiffs could recover an indemnity for what they had spent on rates, rent and repairs under the covenants in the lease, because these expenses arose necessarily out of the contract. It refused to award compensation for other losses, since to do so would be to award damages, not an indemnity, there being no obligation created by the contract to carry on a poultry farm on the premises or to employ a manager, etc.

■ Note – rescission, even if enforced by the court, is always the act of the defrauded party. It is effective from the date it is communicated to the representor or the police (see above) and not from the date of any judgment in subsequent litigation.

Rescission is subject to certain bars

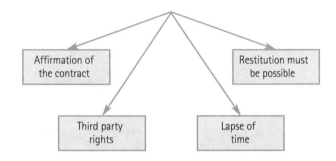

Affirmation of the contract

The representee may not rescind if he has affirmed the contract after learning of the misrepresentation either by declaring his intention to proceed with the contract or by performing some act from which such an intention can be inferred. In *Long v Lloyd* [1958], the buyer of a lorry undertook a long journey after discovering serious defects in the lorry. Held – he had affirmed the contract.

Lapse of time

This can provide evidence of affirmation where the misrepresentee fails to rescind for a considerable time after discovering the falsity.

In cases of innocent misrepresentation, lapse of time can operate as a separate bar to rescission. In *Leaf v International Galleries* [1950], the plaintiff bought a picture which the seller had innocently misrepresented to be by Constable. Five years later, the plaintiff discovered that it was not by Constable and immediately sought to rescind the contract. Held – barred by lapse of time.

Restitution must be possible

A person seeking to rescind the contract must be able and willing to restore what he has received under it. However, rescission is an equitable remedy, and the court will not allow minor failures in the restoration to the original position to stand in the way. In *Erlanger v New Sombrero Phosphate Co* [1878], the purchaser had worked phosphate mines briefly. Held – he could rescind by restoring property and accounting for any profit derived from it. This approach was later followed in *Halpern v Halpern* [2007].

Third party rights

There can be no rescission if third parties have acquired rights in the subject matter of the contract. See *Phillips v Brooks* [1919] and *Lewis v Averay* [1972] – Chapter 6.

MISREPRESENTATION

The requirements of misrepresentation | Remedies for misrepresentation

REPRESENTATIONS AND TERMS OF A CONTRACT

Material statements made during negotiations leading to a contract may be either:

- terms of the contract. If these are untrue, the untruth constitutes a breach of contract; or

- statements which helped to induce the contract, that is, 'mere representations'. If untrue – they are 'misrepresentations'.

(For distinctions between terms and 'mere representations' see Chapter 3.)

REQUIREMENTS OF MISREPRESENTATION

It must be:

> An untrue statement of fact made by one party to the contract (representor) to the other (representee) which induces the other to enter into the contract

A statement of fact

▨ Not a 'mere puff', that is, a statement so vague as to be without effect, for example, describing a house as a 'desirable residence'.

▨ Not a promise. A promise to do something in the future is only actionable if the promise amounts to a binding contract (*Kleinwort Benson Ltd v Malaysian Mining Corpn Bhd* [1989]).

▨ Not a statement of opinion. See below:

▶ BISSET v WILKINSON [1927]

Facts

The vendor of a farm which had never been used as a sheep farm stated that in his judgment the farm would support 2,000 sheep. It transpired that the farm would not support this number of sheep.

Held

The statement was an opinion only. The maker of the statement had no expert knowledge and the farm had never been used for this purpose previously.

But, a statement expressed as an opinion may be treated as a statement of fact if the person making the statement was in a position to know the true facts.

▶ SMITH v LAND AND HOUSE PROP CORPN [1884]

Facts

The vendor of a hotel described it as 'let to a most desirable tenant', when the tenant had for a long time been in arrears with the rent.

Held

There had been a misrepresentation of fact.

▨ Not a statement of intention. But, if the representor did not have that intention, then it is a misstatement of fact, as in *Edgington v Fitzmaurice*

[1885] where the directors issued a prospectus claiming that the money raised was to be used to improve the company's buildings and to expand its business. Their real intention was to pay off the company's debts. Held – fraudulent misrepresentation.

▨ Traditionally, statements of law have not been actionable. However, it may be that statements of law are now actionable as a result of the decision of the House of Lords in *Kleinwort Benson v Lincoln City Council* [1998] (a restitution case so not directly on point, but the implications are clear). This view was adopted in *Pankhania v Hackney LBC* [2002].

An active representation

▨ The statement will normally be in words, but other forms of communication which misrepresent the facts will suffice, as in *Horsfall v Thomas* [1862] (below, p. 83). Thus, misrepresentation may be by conduct.

▶ SPICE GIRLS LTD v APRILIA WORLD SERVICES BV [2000]

Facts

The Spice Girls entered into a sponsorship agreement with Aprilia, a manufacturer of motor scooters, and made a commercial at a time when they knew that Geri Halliwell was about to leave.

Held

This was held to be a misrepresentation that the group did not know and had no reasonable grounds to believe that any member of the group had an intention to leave before the end of the sponsorship agreement.

▨ Failure to make a statement, however, or the non-disclosure of facts, will not generally qualify as misrepresentation.

Exceptions

▨ Where facts have been selected to give a misleading impression.

> ▶ DIMMOCK v HALLETT [1866]
>
> Facts
>
> A vendor of land stated that farms were let, but omitted to say that the tenants had given notice to quit.
>
> Held
>
> The omission of this fact distorted the real picture to the extent that the court found there to be a misrepresentation.

- Where circumstances have changed since a representation was made, then the representor has a duty to correct the statement.

> ▶ WITH v O'FLANAGAN [1936]
>
> Facts
>
> It was stated correctly that a medical practice was worth £2,000 a year, but, the doctor fell ill and most of the clients left the practice. By the time the practice changed hands, it was practically worthless.
>
> Held
>
> Failure by the vendor to disclose the changed circumstances amounted to a misrepresentation.

- Contracts *uberrimae fidei* ('of the utmost good faith'), for example:

  ● Contracts of insurance. Material facts must be disclosed, that is, facts which would influence an insurer in deciding whether to accept the proposal, or to fix the amount of the premium; for example, a policy of life insurance has been voided because it was not disclosed that the proposer had already been turned down by other insurers. The rule exists to prevent one party from having un unfair bargaining position over another, as in this type of contract it is difficult for the other party to find out the relevant facts for themselves. See *International Management Group UK Ltd v Simmonds* [2003].

  ● Family arrangements. In *Gordon v Gordon* [1816–19], a division of property based on the proposition that the elder son was illegitimate was set aside upon proof that the younger son had concealed his knowledge of a private marriage ceremony solemnised before the birth of this brother.

● Analogous contracts, where there is a duty to disclose not material but unusual facts, for example, contracts of suretyship.

● The current law on insurance contracts is currently under review. See Law Commission Consultation Paper: *Contract Law Misrepresentation, Non-disclosure and Breach of Warranty by the Insured* [2007].

For Consumer Contracts, the Commission is advocating that the general duty to volunteer information be abolished and replaced by a requirement to answer questions honestly and reasonably. Under the Law Commission proposals, the duty of disclosure for business insurance contracts would remain.

Inducement

A statement likely to induce a person to contract will normally be assumed to have done so. Moreover, if the claimant can show that he was *in fact* induced, it is no defence to argue that a reasonable person would not have been influenced by the misrepresentation (*Museprime Properties Ltd v Adhill* [1990]). There is no inducement, however, where:

▓ the misrepresentee or his agent actually knew the truth;

▓ the misrepresentee was ignorant of the misrepresentation when the contract was made. In *Horsfall v Thomas* [1862], the vendor of a gun concealed a defect in the gun (misrepresentation by conduct). The buyer, however, bought the gun without examining it. Held – the attempted misrepresentation had not induced the contract;

▓ the misrepresentee did not allow the representation to affect his judgment. In *Attwood v Small* [1838], a buyer appointed an agent to check the statement made by the seller as to the reserves in a mine. Held – not actionable misrepresentation. The buyer had relied on his own agent's statements, not that of the vendor.

Note, however, that:

▓ provided that the representation was one of the inducements, it need not be the sole inducement;

▦ the fact that the representee did not take advantage of an opportunity to check the statement is no bar to an action for misrepresentation.

▶ REDGRAVE v HURD [1881]

Facts

A solicitor was induced to purchase a house and practice by the innocent misrepresentation of the seller. He was invited to check the paperwork relating to the business accounts.

Held

The claimant was entitled to rescission although he did not examine the documents that were available to him and which would have indicated to him the true state of affairs;

▦ neither is it contributory negligence not to check a statement made by a vendor (*Gran Gelato v Richcliff* [1992]).

REMEDIES FOR MISREPRESENTATION

RESCISSION

Misrepresentation renders a contract voidable – see above. The Misrepresentation Act 1967 provides that rescission is available in relation to:

▦ 'executed' contracts for the sale of goods and conveyances of property;

▦ representations which have been incorporated as a term of the contract.

Rescission was not available in these circumstances before 1967.

DAMAGES

▦ There are five ways in which damages may be claimed for misrepresentation. It seems likely that in future the normal ground for damages will be the Misrepresentation Act 1967; but there are still cases where damages can only be claimed at common law, if at all.

▦ Note – rescission and damages are alternative remedies in many cases, but, if the victim of fraudulent or negligent misrepresentation has suffered consequential loss, he may rescind and sue for damages.

▨ Damages can be claimed on different bases, according to the kind of misrepresentation that was committed.

Damages in the tort of deceit for fraudulent misrepresentation

It is up to the misled party to prove that the misrepresentation was made fraudulently, that is, knowingly, without belief in its truth, or recklessly as to whether it be true or false (*Derry v Peek* [1889]).

The burden of proof on the misled party is a heavy one.

Damages in the tort of negligence

Victims of negligent misrepresentation may be able to sue under *Hedley Byrne v Heller & Partners* [1963]. The misrepresentee must prove: (1) that the misrepresentor owed him a duty to take reasonable care in making the representation, that is, there must be a 'special relationship'; (2) that the statement had been made negligently.

Damages under s 2(1) of the Misrepresentation Act 1967

Section 2(1) of the Misrepresentation Act 1967 provides that where a person has entered into a contract after a misrepresentation has been made to him by another party thereto, and as a result of it has suffered loss, 'then, if the misrepresentor would be liable for damages if it had been made fraudulently, he will be so liable notwithstanding that the misrepresentation was not made fraudulently, unless he proves that he had reasonable grounds to believe, and did believe up to the time the contract was made that the facts represented were true'.

Note that this is a more beneficial remedy for the misrepresentee as he only need prove that the statement is untrue. It is for the misrepresentor to prove that he had good grounds for making the statement, and the burden of proof is a heavy one.

▶ HOWARD MARINE AND DREDGING CO LTD v OGDEN [1978]

Facts

The owner of two barges told the hirer that the capacity of the barges was 1,600 tons. He obtained these figures from the Lloyd's list but, in this case, the Lloyd's list was incorrect.

Held

The court determined that he did not have good grounds for this statement; he should have consulted the manufacturer's specifications which should have been in his possession.

Assessment of damages

Damages in the tort of deceit and the tort of negligence are calculated on the basis that the claimant is to be put in the position he was in before the tort was committed ('the reliance basis').

The COA confirmed in *Royscot Trust v Rogerson* [1991] that damages under s 2(1) of the Misrepresentation Act should also be awarded on the reliance basis, because of the 'fiction of fraud' in the wording of the Act.

Remoteness of damage

The COA also held in that case, because of the 'fiction of fraud', that the rules of remoteness which normally apply only to the tort of deceit should be applied under s 2(1):

> That is, damages would be awarded to cover all losses which flow directly from the untrue statement, whether or not those losses were foreseeable

(In contract and in all torts other than deceit, the losses must be 'reasonably foreseeable'.)

▶ ROYSCOT TRUST v ROGERSON [1991]

Facts

A customer arranged to acquire a car on hire purchase from a car dealer. The finance was to be provided by a finance company, the

Royscot Trust, which insisted on a deposit of 20%. The dealer falsified the figures in order to indicate a deposit of 20% as required. Some months later, the customer wrongfully sold the car, thus depriving the finance company of its property. The finance company sued the dealer under s 2(1) of the Misrepresentation Act.

Held

The finance company could recover damages from the car dealer to cover the loss of the car, since the loss followed the misrepresentation. The remoteness rules applicable to the tort of deceit would be applied and the loss did not need to be foreseeable.

Controversy has followed this decision, as the tort of deceit to which this rule only previously applied is difficult to establish and involves moral culpability on the part of the defendant. It has now been extended to an action which is relatively easy to establish (see *Howard Marine and Dredging v Ogden* [1978]) and may only involve carelessness. Some doubts as to whether this was the correct approach were expressed, *obiter*, by the HOL in *Smith New Court Securities Ltd v Scrimgeour Vickers (Asset Management) Ltd* [1996], but for the time being *Royscot v Rogerson* remains good law.

▨ Further problems are caused by the decision of the COA in *East v Maurer* [1991], a case on the tort of deceit, where it was held that 'all damages flowing directly from the fraud' would cover damages for some degree of loss of profit – a heading previously considered to be appropriate only to expectation damages in contract. It is unclear whether the courts will apply this decision to cases under the Misrepresentation Act and bring loss of profit under the heading of reliance loss on the basis that all losses which flow directly from the misrepresentation should be recoverable.

▨ A generous interpretation of s 2(1) of the 1967 Act had also been applied by the court in *Naughton v O'Callaghan* [1990] where reliance damages had been awarded to cover not only the difference between the value of a colt and the value it would have had if the statements made about it were correct (the quantification rule for breach of contract), but also the cost of its maintenance since the sale.

It has been alleged that these three cases swell the amount of damages which can be awarded under the Misrepresentation Act to a greater extent than intended by Parliament, and that the damages available for misrepresentation can now exceed those available for breach of contract.

Damages for wholly innocent misrepresentation

Damages cannot be claimed for a misrepresentation which is neither fraudulent nor negligent, but:

■ An indemnity may be awarded (see *Whittington v Seale-Hayne* [1900]).

■ Damages in lieu of rescission may be awarded under s 2(2) of the Misrepresentation Act 1967.

In *William Sindall v Cambridgeshire CC* [1994], the COA stated (*obiter*) that where the court is considering whether to award damages in lieu of rescission, three matters should be taken into consideration:

● the nature of the misrepresentation;

● the loss which would be caused to the representee if the contract were upheld;

● the hardship caused to the misrepresentor if the contract were rescinded.

The COA also stated that the damages should resemble damages for breach of warranty.

■ There is disagreement as to whether damages can be awarded in lieu even if one of the bars to rescission applies. *Thomas Witter Ltd v TBP Industries* [1996] suggests that they can, whereas *Floods & Queensferry Ltd v Shand Construction Ltd* [2000] and *Government of Zanzibar v British Aerospace (Lancaster House) Ltd* [2000] suggest that they cannot.

■ Where the misrepresentation has become a term of the contract, the misrepresentee can sue for damages for breach of contract, as an alternative to damages for misrepresentation.

Summary of remedies for misrepresentation

Fraudulent	■ Contract voidable ■ Damages in tort of deceit ■ Rescission

Negligent	▨ Contract voidable
	▨ Damages in tort of negligence (*Hedley Byrne v Heller & Partners* [1963])
	▨ Damages s 2(1) Misrepresentation Act 1967
	▨ Rescission
Innocent	▨ Contract voidable
	▨ Rescission
	▨ Damages in lieu of rescission may be awarded – s 2(2) Misrepresentation Act 1967
	▨ Indemnity (*Whittington v Seale-Hayne* [1900])

DURESS

A common law doctrine.

Duress involves coercion

DURESS TO THE PERSON

This requires actual or threatened violence to the person. Originally, it was the only form of duress recognised by the law.

▶ BARTON v ARMSTRONG [1975]

Facts

A Managing Director was threatened with death if he did not purchase the former chairman's shares. The Managing Director was happy to purchase the shares notwithstanding the threats that had been made.

Held

The threats were sufficient to constitute duress and the contract was set aside.

DURESS TO GOODS

▨ Threat of damage to goods – traditionally, this has not been recognised by the law; but, in view of the development of economic duress, it is assumed that duress to goods would today be a ground for relief.

ECONOMIC DURESS

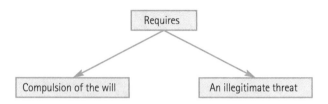

Economic duress led to rescission of a contract in *Universe Tankships of Monrovia v ITWF* [1983] where a union had 'blacked' a tanker, and refused to let it leave port until certain monies had been paid. The HOL considered that this amounted to economic duress and ordered return of the money.

It has been stated that economic duress requires:

Compulsion or coercion of the will

In *Pau On v Lau Yiu Long* [1980], Lord Scarman listed the following indications of compulsion or coercion of the will:

- did the party coerced have an alternative course open to him?;

- did the party coerced protest?;

- did the party coerced have independent advice?;

- did the party coerced take steps to avoid the contract?

Illegitimate pressure

There must be some element of illegitimacy in the pressure exerted, for example, a threatened breach of contract. The illegitimacy will normally arise from the fact that what is threatened is unlawful. In *CTN Cash and Carry v Gallaher* [1994], however, the COA accepted, *obiter*, that an outrageous but technically lawful threat could amount to duress. This possibility has not so far been developed in any later cases.

Economic duress is often pleaded together with lack of consideration in cases where a breach of contract is threatened by the promisor, unless he receives additional payment.

▶ ATLAS EXPRESS v KAFCO [1989]

Facts

Kafco, a small company which imported and distributed basketware, had a contract to supply Woolworths. They contracted with Atlas for delivery of the basketware to Woolworths. The contract commenced, then Atlas discovered they had underpriced the contract, and told Kafco that, unless they paid a minimum sum for each consignment, they would cease to deliver. Kafco were heavily dependent on the Woolworths contract, and knew that a failure to deliver would lead both to the loss of the contract and an action for damages. At that time of the year, they could not find an alternative carrier, and agreed, under protest, to make the extra payments. Atlas sued for Kafco's non-payment.

Held

The agreement was invalid for economic duress, and also for lack of consideration.

▦ Cf *Williams v Roffey Bros* [1989] – Chapter 2.

The following threats are probably not illegitimate (subject to the possibility raised by *CTN Cash and Carry v Gallaher* [1994], discussed above):

▦ a threat not to enter into a contract;

▦ a threat to institute civil proceedings;

▦ a threat to call the police.

Note – not all threatened breaches of contract will amount to economic duress. They will do so only when the threatened party has no reasonable alternative open to him. The normal response to a breach of contract is to sue for damages.

Duress renders a contract voidable. Rescission will normally be sought from the courts. See above.

REMEDIES

▶ NORTH OCEAN SHIPPING CO v HYUNDAI CONSTRUCTION CO, THE ATLANTIC BARON [1979]

Facts

HC agreed to build a tanker for NOSC. After payment of the first instalment HC demanded a 10% increase in price although there was no contractual provision for this. NOSC reluctantly agreed as it needed the ship to complete other contractual commitments. NOSC later sued for the excess payment.

Held

The court found economic duress but refused rescission on the ground that the plaintiff had affirmed the contract.

UNDUE INFLUENCE

An equitable doctrine.

> Pressure not amounting to duress at common law, whereby a party is excluded from the exercise of free and independent judgment

▨ Undue influence is based on the misuse of a relationship of trust or confidence between the parties. Where found, it renders a contract voidable. The innocent party will need to apply to the court for rescission of the contract (see above).

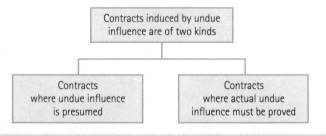

There are two categories of undue influence; actual and presumed.

Actual Undue Influence

This will arise if the claimant can show that they entered a transaction as a result of undue influence exerted by another party. The burden of proof lies on the claimant to show that such influence did exist and was exerted.

CONTRACTS WHERE UNDUE INFLUENCE IS PRESUMED

For example:

- Contracts between certain relationships:

  - parent and child;

  - trustee and beneficiary;

  - solicitor and client;

  - doctor and patient;

  - religious adviser and disciple.

- Where there has been a long relationship of trust and confidence between the parties, and the transaction is not readily explicable by the nature of the relationship. For example, between husband and wife or where one party had been accustomed to rely for guidance and advice on the other. The presumption in these cases of trust and confidence is irrebuttable. The presumption of undue influence, which arises when the transaction 'calls for explanation', is rebuttable.

  In *Credit Lyonnais Bank Nederland NV v Burch* [1997] the relationship between an employer and a junior employee (who was persuaded to put up her own house as security for the business's overdraft) was held to be one of undue influence.

The stronger party can rebut the presumption of undue influence by showing that:

- full disclosure of all material facts was made;

- the consideration was adequate;

- the weaker party was in receipt of independent legal advice.

Manifest Disadvantage

In any claim of presumed undue influence, the agreement must be manifestly disadvantageous. In deciding whether an agreement is manifestly disadvantageous the courts will look at whether the disadvantages of the transaction outweigh the advantages (*Creese v Thomas* [1994]).

EFFECT OF UNDUE INFLUENCE ON A THIRD PARTY

A bank may be deemed to have constructive knowledge of an impropriety if it has been placed 'on inquiry' that one of the parties has unduly influenced the other into entering into the contract.

The leading case on undue influence is *Royal Bank of Scotland v Etridge (No 2)* [2001].

▶ ROYAL BANK OF SCOTLAND v ETRIDGE [2001]

A bank will be placed on inquiry in all cases where the relationship between a debtor and a surety is non-commercial.

Facts

This appeal concerned 8 cases on undue influence. In 7 cases, the wife had permitted the family home, of which she had part ownership to be used as surety against her husband's personal or business debts. In all cases, the husband had defaulted and the bank had sought possession of the family home. The wife claimed that the bank had been placed on inquiry that the agreement had been elicited as a result of the husband's undue influence.

Held

3 appeals were dismissed and 5 were allowed. Moreover, the HOL provided important guidance for banks on how to avoid constructive knowledge of undue influence.

Since the HOL Case of *Royal Bank of Scotland v Etridge (No 2)* [2001] banks are now put on inquiry in every case where the relationship between the surety and the debtor is non-commercial. This will always happen where a wife stands as surety for her husband's debts.

The court in *Royal Bank of Scotland v Etridge* also held that in that situation the third party could discharge his duty by making clear to the party concerned the full nature of the risk he or she is taking on, for example:

- by conducting a personal interview; or

- by urging independent advice.

Note – this doctrine of constructive notice applies to sureties (guarantors) but does not apply where a bank makes a joint loan to both parties as the facts in that situation do not meet the requirements set out in *Barclays Bank v O'Brien*. See *CIBC Mortgages v Pitt* [1993].

- Subsequently, the test laid down in the earlier case of *Barclays Bank v O'Brien* for the third party (bank) to avoid constructive notice has been modified. Where a bank has been put on inquiry, it is not required to have a personal meeting with the guarantor/surety, provided that a suitable alternative (usually a solicitor) is available. Normally, the bank can rely upon the solicitor's confirmation that appropriate advice has been given. Ordinarily, deficiencies in advice are a matter between the solicitor and the guarantor/surety – *Royal Bank of Scotland v Etridge (No 2)* [2001].

- Once undue influence or misrepresentation has been found, the whole contract is avoided; it cannot be upheld in part – *TSB Bank plc v Camfield* [1995].

- Damages are not available as a remedy for duress or undue influence.

You should now be confident that you would be able to tick all of the boxes on the checklist at the beginning of this chapter. To check your knowledge of Vitiating elements which render a contract voidable why not visit the companion website and take the Multiple Choice Question test. Check your understanding of the terms and vocabulary used in this chapter with the flashcard glossary.

6

Mistake

There is much disagreement concerning the effect of mistake on a contract. There are many reasons for this: confusion as to which terms to use; a large number of cases which can be interpreted in different ways; no recent decisive HOL decisions on the subject; the intervention of equity.

TERMINOLOGY

Different terms are used by Cheshire and Anson to describe the same kind of mistake, and you should ascertain which terms are used in your textbook.

	Cheshire	Anson	Effect
Same mistake made by both parties	Common mistake	Mutual mistake	May nullify agreement
Parties at cross-purposes	Mutual mistake	Unilateral mistake	Negates agreement
Parties at cross-purposes, but one party knows that the other is mistaken	Unilateral mistake	Unilateral mistake	Negates agreement

The terms used by Cheshire are used in this *Lawcard*.

In common mistakes, the parties are agreed but both are mistaken

In mutual and unilateral mistakes, the parties may not have reached agreement, and these mistakes are sometimes dealt with under the heading of agreement

EFFECT OF A MISTAKE

The general rule is that a mistake has no effect on a contract, but certain mistakes of a fundamental nature, sometimes called operative mistakes, may render a contract void at common law.

If the contract is rendered void, then the parties will be returned to their original positions, and this may defeat the rights of innocent third parties who may have acquired an interest in the contract.

The reluctance of the courts to develop the common law doctrine of mistake is probably due to the unfortunate consequences for third parties that can result from holding a contract void. Equity at one stage intervened to create a more flexible doctrine, but this has been overruled.

OPERATIVE MISTAKES

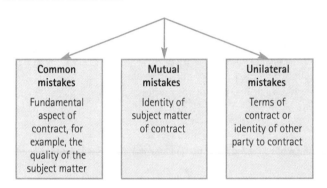

Common mistakes	Mutual mistakes	Unilateral mistakes
Fundamental aspect of contract, for example, the quality of the subject matter	Identity of subject matter of contract	Terms of contract or identity of other party to contract

COMMON MISTAKES

The parties are agreed, but they are both under the same misapprehension. If this misapprehension is sufficiently fundamental, it may nullify the agreement

- At common law, this may render the contract void: that is, the contract has no legal effect; it is unenforceable by either party and title to property cannot pass under it.

- In equity, a more flexible approach has developed; contracts containing certain common mistakes have been treated as voidable. In setting aside such contracts, the courts have a much wider control over the terms they can impose on the parties.

▶ BELL v LEVER BROS [1932]

To nullify the agreement, the 'mistake must go to the root of the contract'.

Facts

Lever Bros agreed to pay two directors of a subsidiary company substantial sums of money in compensation for loss of office, while unaware of the fact that they had engaged in irregular conduct which would have justified their dismissal without compensation. Lever Bros asked the court to order the return of the compensation since it had been paid as a result of a common mistake.

Held

HOL held that the common mistake concerning the need to pay compensation was not 'sufficiently fundamental' to render the contract void. The scope of mistake at common law is therefore very narrow.

Common mistakes 'sufficiently fundamental' to render a contract void

A common mistake as to the existence of the subject matter (res extincta)

▦ In *Galloway v Galloway* [1914], the parties, believing they were married, entered into a separation agreement. Later, they discovered that they were not validly married. Held – the separation agreement was void for a common mistake.

▦ In *Couturier v Hastie* [1856], a buyer bought a cargo of corn which both parties believed to be at sea: the cargo had, however, already been disposed of. Held – the contract was void.

▦ Section 6 of the Sale of Goods Act 1979 declares that: 'Where there is a contract for the sale of specific goods, and the goods without the knowledge of the seller have perished when the contract is made, the contract is void.'

▶ McRAE v COMMONWEALTH DISPOSALS COMMISSION [1951]

Facts

The commission sold to McRae the right to salvage a tanker lying on a specified reef. It later transpired that there was no such reef of that name, nor was there any tanker.

Held

There was a valid contract and the commission had impliedly guaranteed the existence of the tanker. The case could be distinguished from the Australian equivalent of s 6 on the ground that there never had been a tanker and it had, therefore, not perished.

Whether a contract is void or valid depends on the construction of the contract; that is, even if the subject matter does not exist, the contract will be valid:

● if performance was guaranteed; or

● if it was the purchase of a 'chance'.

Otherwise, the contract would be void.

Mistake as to title – res sua – that is, the thing sold already belongs to the buyer

▦ In *Cooper v Phibbs* [1867], Cooper, not realising that a fishery already belonged to him, agreed to lease it from Phibbs. Held – the contract was void.

Mistake as to the quality of the subject matter

Lords Atkin and Thankerton both insisted in *Bell v Lever Bros* that, to render a contract void, the mistake must go to the 'root of the contract'.

▦ It has been argued that if the mistake in *Bell* was not sufficiently fundamental to render a contract void, then it is highly unlikely that any mistake concerning quality would do so.

▦ Similarly, in *Leaf v International Galleries* [1950], where both parties mistakenly believed that a painting was by Constable, the COA stated that the contract was not void for common mistake.

However, Lord Justice Steyn in *Associated Japanese Bank v Credit du Nord* [1988] stated that not enough attention had been paid to speeches in *Bell v Lever Bros* which did indicate that a narrow range of mistakes in quality could render a contract void, for example, Lord Atkin's statement that 'a contract may be void if the mistake is as to the existence of some quality which makes the thing without that quality essentially different from the thing it was believed to be'. He gave as an example – if a horse believed to be sound turns out to be unsound, then the contract remains valid; but, if a horse believed to be a racehorse turns out to be a carthorse, then the contract is void.

EQUITY

For many years, even though the contract was not void at common law, it was potentially voidable in equity as a result of the decision in *Solle v Butcher*. However, in *Great Peace Shipping Ltd v Tsavliris Salvage (International) Ltd* [2002], the COA decided that *Solle v Butcher* was decided *per incuriam* and that there is no equitable jurisdiction to grant rescission of a contract on the ground of common mistake when that contract is valid at common law.

MUTUAL AND UNILATERAL MISTAKES

These mistakes negate consent; that is, they prevent the formation of an agreement

The courts adopt an objective test in deciding whether agreement has been reached. It is not enough for one of the parties to allege that he was mistaken.

Mistake can negate consent in the following cases.

Mutual mistakes concerning the identity of the subject matter

In these cases the parties are at cross-purposes, but there must have been some ambiguity in the situation before the courts will declare the contract void

❯ RAFFLES v WICHELHAUS [1864]

Facts

A consignment of cotton was bought to arrive 'ex *Peerless* from Bombay'. Two ships, both called *Peerless* were due to leave Bombay at around the same time.

Held

No agreement as the buyer was thinking of one ship, and the seller was referring to the other ship.

- Similarly, there was no agreement in *Scriven Bros v Hindley & Co Ltd* [1913] where the seller sold 'tow' and the buyer bought 'hemp'. Again, there was an ambiguity as both lots were delivered under the same shipping mark and the catalogue was vague.

- But, in *Smith v Hughes* [1871], the court refused to declare void an agreement whereby the buyer had thought he was buying old oats when in fact they were new oats, as the contract was for the sale of 'oats'. The mistake related to the quality not the identity of the subject matter.

Unilateral mistake concerning the terms of the contract

Here, one party has taken advantage of the other party's error

❯ HARTOG v COLIN AND SHIELDS [1939]

Facts

The sellers mistakenly offered to sell goods at a given price per pound when they intended to offer them per piece. All the preliminary negotiations had been on a per piece basis. The buyers must have realised that the sellers had made a mistake.

Held

The contract was declared void.

- In *Smith v Hughes*, however, the contract was for the sale of 'oats' not 'old

103

oats'; it would only have been void if 'old oats' had been a term of the contract.

Unilateral mistake as to the identity of other parties to the contract

There are a number of contradictory cases and theories under this heading. Traditionally, a distinction is made between mistakes as to identity and mistakes as to attributes (for example, credit-worthiness). Where the identity of the other party is if of fundamental importance, and there has been a genuine mistake, the contract will be void

▶ CUNDY v LINDSAY [1878]

Facts

A Mr Blenkarn ordered goods from Lindsay signing the letter to give the impression that the order came from Blenkiron & Co, a firm known to Lindsay & Co.

Held

The contract was void. Lindsay & Co had only intended to do business with Blenkiron & Co. There was therefore a mistake concerning the identity of the other party to the contract.

A mistake as to attributes or credit-worthiness will not render a contract void

▶ KING'S NORTON METAL CO v EDRIDGE MERRETT & CO LTD [1872]

Facts

A Mr Wallis ordered goods on impressive stationery which indicated that the order had come from Hallam & Co, an old established firm with branches all over the country.

Held

The contract was not void. The sellers intended to do business with the writer of the letter; they were merely mistaken as to his attributes, that is, the size and credit-worthiness of his business.

▶ BOULTON v JONES [1857]

Facts

The defendant sent an order for some goods to a Mr Brocklehurst unaware that he had sold the business to his foreman, the plaintiff. The plaintiff supplied the goods but the defendant refused to pay for them as he had only intended to do business with Brocklehurst, against whom he had a set off.

Held

There was a mistake concerning the identity of the other party and the contract was therefore void.

▶ SHOGUN FINANCE LTD v HUDSON [2003]

Facts

A rogue, calling himself Patel, went into a motor dealer's and set up a hire-purchase contract to buy a new car. The finance company (with whom the contract was made) relied upon information from a driving licence (genuine, but stolen) produced to the dealer by the rogue, in the name of Durlabh Patel; it also checked the name and address in the electoral register and credit-worthiness. The HP forms were completed in the name of Durlabh Patel; the rogue paid a deposit in cash and by cheque which was ultimately dishonoured, drove the vehicle away and sold it to Hudson, who purchased in good faith.

Held

HOL held that the finance company was able to recover the cost of the vehicle from Hudson. The dealer was not the agent of the finance company; hence this was not a face to face transaction. On the authority of *Hector v Lyons* [1989], where a contract is in writing, the parties to that contract are *prima facie* the persons described as such in the writing, and consequently the HP agreement, if made with anyone, was made with Durlabh Patel, and was void for mistaken identity.

From the above four cases, it would seem that a contract is void if the mistaken party intended to do business with another specific person, and the identity of that other person was important to him

However, the cases all concerned contracts negotiated at a distance.

Where the parties negotiate in person, the same rules apply, but there is a presumption that the innocent party intended to do business with the person physically in his presence

▶ PHILLIPS v BROOKS [1919]

Facts

A jeweller sold a gold ring and delivered it on credit to a customer who had come into his shop and had falsely claimed to be Sir George Bullough, a well known and wealthy man.

Held

The contract was valid. The jeweller had intended to do business with the person in his shop.

▶ LEWIS v AVERAY [1972]

Facts

A rogue claimed to be Richard Greene the film actor and produced a pass to Pinewood studios to verify this. He was allowed to drive away a car in return for a cheque and subsequently resold the car for cash to Averay. The cheque bounced, and the seller claimed the return of the car on the ground that he was mistaken as to the identity of the buyer.

Held

The contract was valid. The seller must be presumed to have intended to deal with the person physically in the room with him. Averay kept the car.

In some cases, however, plaintiffs have been able to establish a mistake as to the identity of a person in their presence.

▶ INGRAM v LITTLE [1961]

Facts

Two sisters sold a car and handed it over against a worthless cheque to a person who claimed to be a Mr Hutchinson of Stanstead House, Caterham. They only did so after one of them had checked that there was a man of that name who lived at that address.

Held

COA held the contract void. The sisters had done enough to establish that they only intended to deal with Mr Hutchinson.

This case has been greatly criticised as it is difficult to reconcile with *Phillips v Brooks* and *Lewis v Averay*.

The contract would in most cases be voidable in any case for misrepresentation where one party has misled the other with regard to his identity. The advantage of having the contract declared void for mistake is to avoid the bars to rescission.

See Chapter 5.

MISTAKE IN EQUITY

The narrow approach taken by the common law towards remedies for mistake (that is, that it renders the contract void) is supplemented by the more flexible approach of equity. The following remedies may be available in equity:

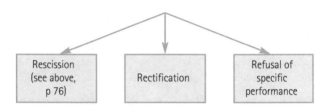

| Rescission (see above, p 76) | Rectification | Refusal of specific performance |

Rectification

Where there has been a mistake, not in the actual agreement but in reducing it to writing, equity will order rectification of the document so that it coincides with the true agreement of the parties.

Necessary conditions

▪ The document does not represent the intention of both parties; or

▪ one party mistakenly believed that a term was included in the document, and the other party knew of this error. In *Roberts & Co Ltd v Leicestershire CC* [1961], the completion date of a contract was rectified at the request of one party because it was clear that the other party was aware of the error when the contract was signed.

If the document fails to mention a term which one party but not the other had intended to be a term of the contract, there is no case for rectification.

▪ There must have been a concluded agreement, but not necessarily a legally enforceable contract. In *Joscelyne v Nissen* [1970], a father and daughter agreed that the daughter should take over the car hire business. In return, the father would continue to live in the house and the daughter would pay all the household expenses. This last provision was not included in the written contract. Held – the contract should be rectified to include it.

Note – a document which accurately records a prior agreement cannot be rectified because the agreement was made under some mistake (*Rose v Pym*, above). Equity rectifies documents not agreements.

Rectification is an equitable remedy and is available at the discretion of the court. Lapse of time or conflict with third party rights may prevent rectification.

Refusal of specific performance

Specific performance will be refused when the contract is void at common law. Equity may also refuse specific performance where a contract is valid at law, but only 'where a hardship amounting to injustice would have been inflicted upon him by holding him to his bargain' (*Tamplin v James* [1879]).

■ In *Webster v Cecil* [1861], the defendant, having previously refused the plaintiff's offer of £2,000 for his land, wrote to the plaintiff offering to sell it to him for £1,250 instead of £2,250 as he had intended. The plaintiff accepted the offer. Specific performance was refused as the plaintiff must have been aware of the error (unilateral mistake).

You should now be confident that you would be able to tick all of the boxes on the checklist at the beginning of this chapter. To check your knowledge of Mistake why not visit the companion website and take the Multiple Choice Question test. Check your understanding of the terms and vocabulary used in this chapter with the flashcard glossary.

7

Illegality and capacity

Illegal contracts are classified in different ways by different authorities. In this chapter, a distinction is drawn between contracts which involve the commission of a common law or statutory offence, and those that are void as being contrary to public policy.

ILLEGALITY

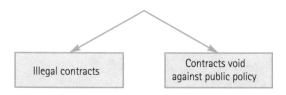

The main issue with regard to illegal contracts is the effect of illegality on a contract. The most often examined topic with regard to contracts which are declared void on grounds of public policy is contracts in restraint of trade.

ILLEGAL CONTRACTS

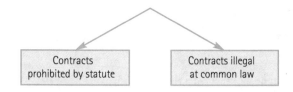

Contracts illegal by statute

- Statute may declare a contract illegal, for example, the Competition Act 1998.

- Statute may prohibit an act, but declare that it shall not affect validity of contract, for example, the Consumer Protection Act 1987.

- Statute may prohibit an act but not stipulate its effect on the contract. The status of the contract will in this case be a matter of interpretation for the court. In *Re Mahmoud and Ispahani* [1921], the court decided that a statement that 'a person shall not buy or otherwise deal in linseed oil without a licence' was a prohibition, and a contract entered into by a person without a licence was therefore void.

- The courts are reluctant to imply a prohibition when this is not clearly indicated in the statute. In *Hughes v Asset Managers* [1995], the court held a contract valid despite the fact that a document had not been signed by a person authorised to do so as required by statute.

Contracts illegal at common law

- An agreement to commit a crime, a tort or a fraud.
- An agreement to defraud the Inland Revenue (*Napier v Business Associates* [1951]).
- Contracts damaging to the country's safety or foreign relations.
- Contracts interfering with the course of justice, for example, contracts to give false evidence.
- Contracts leading to corruption in public life (*Parkinson v Royal College of Ambulance* [1925]).
- Contracts tending to promote sexual immorality (*Pearce v Brooks* [1866]).

EFFECTS OF ILLEGALITY

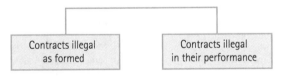

Contracts illegal as formed

> Such contracts are void *ab initio*: there can be no action for breach of contract

In *Pearce v Brooks* [1866], the owner of a coach of unusual design was unable to recover the cost of hire from a prostitute who, to his knowledge, had hired it in order to attract clients.

> Money paid, or property transferred, under the contract cannot be recovered

In *Parkinson v Royal College of Ambulance* [1925], Parkinson was unable to recover the money he had donated to the defendants on the understanding that they would obtain a knighthood for him.

Exceptions

- Where the parties are not equally at fault, for example, where one party is unaware of the illegal nature of the contract.

- Where the transferor genuinely repents and repudiates the contract before performance. In *Tribe v Tribe* [1995], money was transferred to a son in order to avoid the father's creditors. Ultimately, the creditors were all paid in full, and the father was allowed to cite the original reason for the transfer in order to rebut the presumption of advancement (which would have meant that his son could keep the shares). He had withdrawn from the illegal purpose before performance.

  In *Bigos v Boustead* [1951], however, the court was not convinced that the plaintiff had genuinely repented.

- Where the transferor can frame his claim without relying on the contract. In *Bowmakers v Barnet Instruments* [1945], the plaintiffs were able to rely on an action in the tort of conversion to recover goods delivered under an illegal hire purchase contract.

  Similarly, in *Tinsley v Milligan* [1993], both parties had contributed money towards the purchase of a house put in the name of Tinsley alone in order to allow Milligan to make various social security claims. When Milligan sued for the return of the money, it was argued that the agreement had been entered into for an illegal purpose and that the public conscience 'would be affronted by recognising rights created by illegal transactions'. The HOL held, however, that a resulting trust had been created in favour of Milligan by the contribution to the purchase price. Milligan, therefore could rely on the resulting trust and had no need to rely on the illegal agreement.

  This case shows: (a) that the rule applies to equity as well as to common law; (b) that the test of 'affront to the public conscience' previously used by the COA is no longer good law.

- Where part of the contract is lawful, the court will not sever the good from the bad. In *Napier v National Business Agency* [1951], certain payments were described as 'expenses' in order to defraud the Inland Revenue. The court refused to enforce payment of the accompanying salary, as the whole contract was tainted with the illegality.

Note – property can pass under an illegal contract, as in *Sing v Ali* [1960].

Contracts illegal in their performance

> The illegality may only arise during the performance of a contract, for example, a carrier may break the law by exceeding the speed limit whilst delivering goods belonging to a client. He will be punished, but the contract will not necessarily be void

A claim by the innocent party to enforce the contract in these circumstances is likely to succeed.

- In *Marles v Philip Trant* [1954], the defendant sold winter wheat described as spring wheat, without an accompanying invoice as required by statute. Held – the plaintiff could sue for damages for breach of contract. The contract was illegal in its performance, but not in its formation.

- In *Strongman v Sincock* [1955], Sincock failed to get licences which were needed to modernise some houses which belonged to him, and refused to pay for the work on the basis that the contracts were illegal. Held – Strongman could not sue on the illegal contracts, but could sue Sincock on his collateral promise to obtain the licences.

- In *Archbolds v Spanglett* [1961], Spanglett contracted to carry Archbolds whisky in a van which was not licensed to carry any goods other than his own. Archbold was unaware of this and could therefore recover damages for breach of contract.

  But, in *Ashmore, Benson, Pease & Co v Dawson Ltd* [1973], the other party knew of the overloading of the lorry, and could not, therefore, recover damages. He had participated in the illegality.

■ Even the guilty party may enforce the contract, if the illegality is incidental.

In *Shaw v Groom* [1970], a landlord failed to give his tenant a rent book as required by law. Held – he could sue for the rent. The purpose of the statute was to punish the landlord's failure to provide a rent book, not to render the contract void.

In *St John Shipping v Rank* [1957], a ship owner who had overloaded his ship in contravention of a statute was able to recover freight.

CONTRACTS VOID AT COMMON LAW ON GROUNDS OF PUBLIC POLICY

Contracts damaging to the institution of marriage.

For example, contracts in restraint of marriage, marriage brokerage contracts, contracts for future separation (pre-nuptial agreements).

Contracts made after or immediately before separation are valid

Contracts to oust the jurisdiction of the courts

However, arbitration agreements are valid

CONTRACTS IN RESTRAINT OF TRADE

A contract in restraint of trade is *prima facie* void, but the courts will now uphold the restriction if it is shown that:

■ the restraint protects a legitimate interest;
■ the restraint is reasonable between the parties;

■ the restraint is reasonable as regards the interest of the public.

In *Esso Petroleum v Harpers Garage* [1968], it was stated that the court will consider:

■ whether the contract is in restraint of trade. A contract is in restraint of trade if it restricts a person's liberty to carry on his trade or profession. Certain restraints have become acceptable over the years, for example, 'tied houses', restrictive covenants in leases, sole agency, or sole distributorship agreements;

■ whether it should nevertheless be enforced because it protects a legitimate interest and is reasonable. The onus of proving reasonability is on the promisee. A restraint, to be permissible, must be no wider than is necessary to protect the legitimate interest of the promisee.

Categories of contracts in restraint of trade

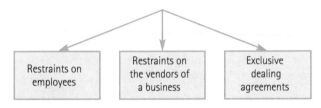

Restraints on employees

Restraints on the vendors of a business

Exclusive dealing agreements

Restraints on employees
The restraint is void, unless the employer can show:

■ That it is necessary to protect a proprietary interest, for example, the trade secrets of a works manager in *Forster v Suggett* [1918]; the trade connections of a solicitor's managing clerk in *Fitch v Dewes* [1921].

▶ FORSTER v SUGGETT [1918]

Facts
The contracts of certain employees of a glass manufacturing company contained a clause preventing employees from working for any competitors if they left the company.

Held

The clause was upheld. The skill was so specialist in nature that it constituted a trade secret.

▶ FITCH v DEWES [1921]

Facts

A solicitors clerk was prevented from working within a seven mile radius of Tamworth town hall.

Held

The clause was reasonable, given the nature of the practice and the number of potential clients.

A restraint merely to prevent competition will not be enforced.

In *Eastham v Newcastle United FC* [1964], the court accepted that the proper organisation of football was a valid matter for clubs to protect, but found the 'retain and transfer system' unreasonable.

▦ That the restraint is no greater than is necessary to protect the employer's interest in terms of time and area.

In *Scorer v Seymore-Jones* [1966], the court upheld a restriction of 10 miles within branch A at which the employee had worked, but held that a similar restraint covering branch B at which the employee had not worked was unreasonable and void.

▦ Problems with area can be overcome by using 'non-solicitation' clauses instead.

In *Home Counties Dairies v Skilton* [1970], a milkman agreed that, for one year after leaving his present job, he would not sell milk to his employer's customers. Held – restraint valid.

It was necessary to protect the employer against loss of customers.

▦ The validity of the duration of the restraint depends on the nature of the business to be protected, and on the status of the employee.

In *Briggs v Oates* [1991], a restriction of five miles for five years on an assistant solicitor was upheld as reasonable.

▨ A restraint imposed by indirect means, for example, by loss of pension rights (*Bull v Pitney Bowes* [1966]), or where two companies agreed not to take on the other's employees (*Kores v Kolok* [1959]) will be judged by the same criteria.

Restraints on the vendor of a business

> Such a restraint is valid if it is intended to protect the purchaser's interest in the goodwill of the business bought, and is reasonable

▨ In *Vancouver Malt and Sake Brewing Co v Vancouver Breweries Ltd* [1934], a company which was licensed to brew beer, but which had not at any time brewed beer, was sold, and agreed not to brew any beer for 15 years. Held – the restraint was void since there was no goodwill of a beer brewing business to be transferred.

▨ In *British Concrete v Schelff* [1921], S sold his localised business to B who had branches all over the UK and agreed not to open any business within 10 miles of any of B's branches. Held – the restriction was void. B was entitled only to protect the business he had bought not the business which he already owned.

▨ In *Nordenfelt v Maxim Nordenfelt* [1894], N, a worldwide supplier of guns, sold his worldwide business to M, and agreed not to manu-facture guns anywhere in the world for 25 years. Held – the restriction was valid.

Exclusive dealing agreements

> *Solus* agreements, whereby A agrees to buy all his requirements of a particular commodity from B

▨ In *Esso Petroleum v Harpers Garage* [1968], a *solus* agreement for four years was held reasonable, but a solus agreement for 21 years was held unreasonable, and therefore void.

- *Solus* agreements were distinguished from restrictive covenants in a lease. When an oil company leases a filling station to X, inserting a clause that X should buy all its requirements from the company, this is not subject to restraint of trade rules because the tenant is not giving up a previously held freedom.

- But, in *Amoco v Rocca Bros* [1975], the court held that restraint of trade rules did apply to lease and lease-back agreements.

- In *Alec Lobb (Garages) v Total Oil* [1985], in a similar lease-back arrangement, a *solus* agreement for between seven and 21 years was held reasonable on the ground that the arrangement was a rescue operation benefiting the plaintiffs, and there were 'break' clauses in the underlease.

> Most exclusive services contracts are found in professional sport or entertainment

- In *Schroeder Music Publishing Co v Macaulay* [1974], it was held that a contract by which an unknown song writer undertook to give his exclusive services to a publisher who made no promise to publish his work was subject to the restraint of trade doctrine, as it was 'capable of enforcement in an oppressive manner'.

- In *Greig v Insole* [1978], the MCC banned any cricketer who played for a cricketing 'circus' from playing for England. The court held that the ban was void as being in restraint of trade.

It has been suggested that the courts will hold exclusive dealing and service contracts to be within the restraint of trade doctrine if they contain unusual or novel features, or if there is disparity in the bargaining power, and the agreement is likely to cause hardship to the weaker party.

Cartel agreements

These are now covered by statute: for example, the Fair Trading Act 1973 and the Competition Act 1998. Cartel agreements may also fall within Art 81 of the EC Treaty.

A void restraint is severable. Severance can be operated in two ways:

■ severance of the whole of the objectionable promise, leaving the rest of the contract to be enforced
■ severance of the objectionable part of the promise

Effect of a restraint

Two tests must be satisfied:

■ The 'blue pencil' test. It must be possible to sever the illegal part simply by deleting words in the contract. The court will not add words, substitute one word for another, rearrange words or in any way redraft the contract. In *Mason v Provident Clothing Co Ltd* [1913], the HOL refused to redraft a promise not to work within 25 miles of London. But, in *Goldsoll v Goldman* [1915], a dealer in imitation jewellery promised not to deal in real or imitation jewellery either in the UK or abroad. Dealing in real jewellery and dealing abroad were severed.

■ Severance of the objectionable part of the contract must not alter the nature (as distinct from the extent) of the original contract. The illegal restraint will not be severed if it is the main purpose of the restraint, or if to sever it would alter entirely the scope and intention of the agreement. In *Attwood v Lamont* [1920], the court refused to sever restrictions on a tailor from competing with any department of the department store which had employed him. The court stated that this was a covenant 'which must stand or fall in its unaltered form'.

CAPACITY

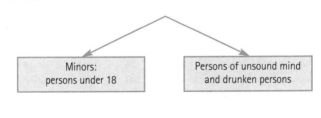

| Minors: persons under 18 | Persons of unsound mind and drunken persons |

MINORS

The law pursues two conflicting policies in the case of minors. On the one hand it tries to protect minors from their own inexperience; on the other, it tries to ensure that persons dealing with minors are not dealt with in a harsh manner.

Contracts with minors can be divided into three categories.

Valid contracts – contracts which can be enforced against a minor

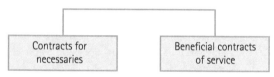

Necessaries

> Necessary goods are defined in the Sale of Goods Act 1979 as 'goods suitable to his condition in life, and to his actual requirements at the time of sale and delivery'

▶ NASH v INMAN [1908]

Facts

A student purchased 11 silk waistcoats while still a minor. He argued that they comprised 'goods suitable to his condition in life, and to his actual requirements at the time of sale and delivery'.

Held

The silk waistcoats were suitable to the conditions of life of a Cambridge undergraduate at that time, but they were not suitable to his actual needs as he already had a sufficient supply of waistcoats.

It is important to distinguish between luxurious goods of utility, and goods of pure luxury. The status of the minor can make the former into necessaries, but the latter can never be classified as necessaries.

The burden of proving that the goods are necessaries is on the seller.

> ### ▶ PROFORM SPORTS MANAGEMENT LTD v PROACTIVE SPORTS MANAGEMENT LTD AND ANOTHER [2006]
>
> #### Facts
> The footballer Wayne Rooney signed a two year management and agency agreement with the claimant when he was aged 15. Rooney later terminated the contract.
>
> #### Held
> The agreement was not a contract of apprenticeship, education or service substantially to the footballer's benefit, thus he was entitled to avoid it.

Necessary services include education, medical and legal services.

They must satisfy the same tests as necessary goods.

Professor Treitel considers that both executed and unexecuted contracts for necessaries can be enforced. He cites *Roberts v Gray* [1913]. Roberts agreed to take Gray, a minor, on a billiard tour to instruct him in the profession of billiard player. Gray repudiated the contract. The court held that Roberts could recover damages despite the fact that the contract was executory.

Cheshire, Fifoot and Furmston agree that executory contracts for necessary services are enforceable as in *Roberts v Gray* but deny that executory contracts for necessary goods can be enforced.

They cite:

- the actual wording of the Sale of Goods Act 1979 which refers to time of 'sale and delivery';

- the minor has to pay a reasonable price for the goods, not the contractual price.

These indicate, it is argued, that liability is based on acceptance of the goods, not on agreement.

Beneficial contracts of service

> These must be for the benefit of the minor

- In *De Francesco v Barnum* [1890], a contract whose terms were burdensome and harsh on the minor was held void.

- But, in *White City Stadium v Doyle* [1935], where a minor had forfeited his payment for a fight because of disqualification, the contract was nevertheless enforceable against him. Where a contract is on the whole for the benefit of a minor, it will not be invalidated because one term has operated in a way which is not to his advantage.

They must be contracts of service or similar to a contract of service.

- In *Chaplin v Leslie Frewin (Publishers) Ltd* [1966], the court enforced a contract by a minor to publish his memoirs as this would train him in becoming an author, and enable him to earn a living.

- But, trading contracts (involving the minor's capital) will not be enforced even if it does help the minor earn a living. In *Mercantile Union Guarantee Co Ltd v Ball* [1937], the court refused to enforce a hire purchase contract for a lorry which would enable a minor to trade as a haulage contractor.

Voidable contracts

> Contracts that can be avoided by the minor before majority or shortly afterwards

These comprise contracts of continuing obligation such as contracts to acquire an interest in land, or partly paid shares, or partnership agreements.

The minor can free himself from obligations for the future, for example, an obligation to pay rent under a lease, but will have to pay for benefits already received. He cannot recover money already paid under the contract unless there has been a total failure of consideration (*Steinberg v Scala (Leeds) Ltd* [1923]).

Other contracts

> These cannot be enforced against a minor

But:

▦ The minor himself may enforce such contracts.

▦ Property can pass under such contracts.

▦ Where the contract has been carried out by the minor, he cannot recover any property unless there has been a total failure of consideration, or some other failing which would equally apply to an adult.

▦ The Minors Contracts Act 1987 provides that:

● a minor may ratify such a contract on majority, and it can thereafter be enforced against him;

● a guarantee of a minor's debt will not be void because a minor's debt is unenforceable against him;

● a court may, if it considers it is just and equitable to do so, order a minor to return property he has received under a void contract or any property representing it. It is not clear whether property transferred under the contract covers money, for example, in money lending contracts.

It is argued that as 'property representing it' must cover money, it would therefore be illogical to exclude money acquired directly, but there is as yet no decision on this point. Property cannot presumably be recovered under this section where the minor has given away the contract property.

▦ Equity will order restitution of property acquired by fraud. But, there can be no restitution of money (*Leslie v Sheill* [1914]) and no restitution if the minor has resold the property.

▦ An action may be brought in tort if it does not in any way rely on the contract. But, although a minor is fully liable for all his torts, he may not be sued in tort if this is just an indirect way of enforcing a contract. In *Leslie v Sheill* [1914], a minor obtained a loan by fraudulently misrepresenting his age. Held – he could not be sued in the tort of deceit as this would be an indirect way of enforcing a contract which was void.

PERSONS OF UNSOUND MIND AND DRUNKEN PERSONS

A person who has been declared a 'patient' under the Mental Health Act 1983 by the Court of Protection is incapable of entering into a valid contract.

Other mentally disordered persons and drunken persons will be bound by their contracts unless:

■ they were so disordered or drunk that they did not understand the nature of what they were doing; and
■ the other party was aware of this.

Such contracts may be affirmed during a sober or lucid moment. The Sale of Goods Act 1979 requires that where 'necessaries are sold and delivered to a person who by reason of mental incapacity or drunkenness is incompetent to contract, he must pay a reasonable price for them'.

You should now be confident that you would be able to tick all of the boxes on the checklist at the beginning of this chapter. To check your knowledge of Illegality and capacity why not visit the companion website and take the Multiple Choice Question test. Check your understanding of the terms and vocabulary used in this chapter with the flashcard glossary.

8

Discharge

A contract is 'discharged' when there are no obligations outstanding under it

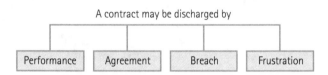

A contract may be discharged by

| Performance | Agreement | Breach | Frustration |

PERFORMANCE

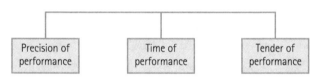

| Precision of performance | Time of performance | Tender of performance |

PRECISION OF PERFORMANCE

To discharge his obligations under a contract, a party must perform exactly what he promised

▶ CUTTER v POWELL [1795]

Facts

A ship's engineer undertook to sail a ship from Jamaica to Liverpool, but died before the voyage was complete. His widow tried to recover wages for work carried out before his death.

Held

Nothing could be recovered in respect of his service; he had not fulfilled his obligation.

Similarly:

❭ BOLTON v MAHADEVA [1972]

Facts
A central heating system gave out less heat than it should, and there were fumes in one room.

Held
The contractor could not claim payment; although the boiler and pipes had been installed, they did not fulfil the primary purpose of heating the house.

These are examples of 'entire' contracts, which consist of one unseverable obligation.

Despite the rule that performance must be exact, the law will allow payment to be made, on a *quantum meruit* basis, for incomplete performance in the following circumstances:

- Where the contract is divisible, payment can be recovered for the completed part, for example, goods delivered by instalments.

- Where the promisee accepts partial performance. In *Sumpter v Hedges* [1898], however, payment for partial performance was refused as Hedges had been left with a half-built house, and had been put in a position where he had no choice but to accept partial performance.

- Where the promisee prevents complete performance. For example, in *Planché v Colburn* [1831], a writer was allowed payment for the work he had already done when the publisher abandoned the series.

- Where the promisor has performed a substantial part of the contract. In *Hoenig v Isaacs* [1952], the plaintiff decorated the defendant's flat, but, because of faulty workmanship, the defendant had to pay £50 to another firm to finish the job. Held – the plaintiff was entitled to £150 (the contract price) minus the £50 paid to the other firm; cf *Bolton v Mahadeva* [1972] where the court declined to find substantial performance.

This has become known as the doctrine of substantial performance. In order for the claimant to rely on this doctrine, the failure to perform must amount only to a breach of warranty or a non-fundamental breach of an innominate term. It will not apply to a fundamental breach or to a breach of condition.

TIME OF PERFORMANCE

Equity considers that time is not 'of the essence of a contract', that is, a condition, except in the following circumstances:

- It is stipulated in the contract: see *Lombard North Central v Butterworth* [1987].

- One party has given reasonable notice during the currency of the contract that performance must take place within a certain time. In *Rickards v Oppenheim* [1950], a car body which had been ordered from the plaintiffs was late. The defendants gave final notice to the plaintiff that unless it was delivered within three months they would cancel the order. Held – time had been made of the essence; the defendants could cancel the order.

- The nature of the contract makes it imperative that stipulations as to time should be observed, for example, contracts for the sale of perishable goods.

- The *Law of Property Act 1925* stipulated that terms as to the time of performance should be interpreted in the same way at common law as in equity. In *Rainieri v Miles* [1981], the HOL held that that meant that late performance would not give rise to a right to terminate, but would give rise to damages.

TENDER OF PERFORMANCE

If one party tenders performance which is refused, he may sue for breach of contract.

If payment is tendered and rejected, the obligation to tender payment is discharged, but the obligation to pay remains.

AGREEMENT

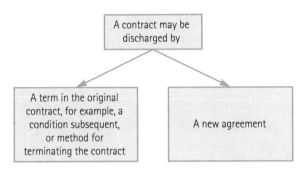

As contracts are created by agreement, so they may be discharged by agreement. Consideration is necessary to make the agreement binding

- If the contract is wholly executory, there is no problem with consideration as both parties surrender their rights under the contract.

- If the contract is partly executed, one party has completed his performance under the contract – to make the agreement binding there must either be a deed (a 'release') or new consideration ('accord and satisfaction'), or the doctrine of equitable estoppel or waiver must apply. See Chapter 2.

BREACH

A breach does not of itself discharge a contract. It may allow the other party an option to treat the contract as discharged, that is, to terminate the contract, if the breach is sufficiently serious: that is, if it is:

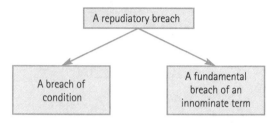

See classification of terms, p 50 above.

There are special problems where a party repudiates a contract under a wrong assumption that he has a right to do so.

> **FEDERAL COMMERCE AND NAVIGATION v MOLENA ALPHA [1979]**

Facts

The owners of a ship gave instructions not to issue bills of lading without which the charterers could not operate the ship. They wrongly believed that they had the right to do so.

Held

Their conduct constituted a wrongful repudiation of the contract which allowed the other party to treat the contract as discharged.

> **WOODAR INVESTMENT DEVELOPMENT v WIMPEY CONSTRUCTION [1980]**

Facts

The purchaser wrongly repudiated a contract for the sale of land, wrongly believing that he had a right to do so.

Held

A wrongful repudiation made in good faith would not necessarily allow the other party to treat the contract as discharged.

It is difficult to distinguish these decisions. The general view is that the approach in *Molena Alpha* is to be preferred, so that even a good faith 'repudiatory' response to a non-repudiatory breach will amount to a breach of contract.

EFFECT OF TREATING THE CONTRACT AS DISCHARGED
The obligation of both parties to perform (that is, the primary obligation) is discharged from the date of the termination.

However, the party in breach may have to pay damages for any losses, past and future, caused to the innocent party as a result of the breach (*Lombard North Central v Butterworth* – Chapter 3).

The discharge does not operate retrospectively. In *Photo Production v Securicor* [1980], Securicor was able to rely on an exclusion clause in the contract, despite the fact that the contract had been discharged.

Note – it was held by the HOL in *Vitol v Norelf* [1996] that the defendant's failure to perform his own obligation could constitute acceptance of the plaintiff's repudiation.

The decision to terminate cannot be retracted.

ANTICIPATORY BREACH OF CONTRACT

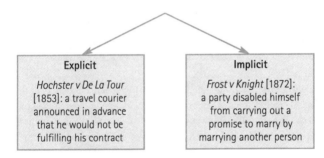

Explicit

Hochster v De La Tour [1853]: a travel courier announced in advance that he would not be fulfilling his contract

Implicit

Frost v Knight [1872]: a party disabled himself from carrying out a promise to marry by marrying another person

Effect of anticipatory breach

- The other party may sue for damages immediately. He does not have to await the date of performance (*Hochster v De La Tour* [1853]).

- The innocent party may refuse to accept the repudiation. He may affirm the contract and continue to perform his obligations under the contract.

❯ WHITE AND CARTER LTD v McGREGOR [1962]

Facts

The defendants cancelled a contract shortly after it had been signed. The plaintiffs refused to accept the cancellation, carried on with the contract, and then sued for the full contract price.

Held

The plaintiffs were entitled to succeed; a repudiation does not automatically bring a contract to an end; the innocent party has an option either to affirm the contract or to terminate.

Unless:

● the innocent party needs the co-operation of the other party.

In *Hounslow BC v Twickenham Garden Developments Ltd* [1971], Hounslow council cancelled a contract to lay out a park. It was held that the defendants could not rely on *White and Carter v McGregor* because the work was to be performed on council property;

● the innocent party had no legitimate interest, financial or otherwise, in performing the contract rather than in claiming damages.

❯ THE ALASKAN TRADER [1984]

Facts

A ship chartered to the defendants required extensive repairs at the end of the first year, whereupon the defendants repudiated the contract. The plaintiffs, however, refused to accept the repudiation, repaired the ship, and kept it fully crewed ready for the defendant's use.

Held

The plaintiffs had no special interest in keeping the contract alive. They should have accepted the repudiation and sued for damages.

This is subject to the claimant's duty to mitigate his loss.

Where a party has affirmed the contract

- He will have to pay damages for any subsequent breach which he commits; he cannot argue that the other party's anticipatory breach excuses him (*Fercometal SARL v Mediterranean Shipping Co* [1988]).

- There is a danger that a supervening event may frustrate the contract and deprive the innocent party of his right to damages, as in *Avery v Bowden* [1855] (below, p. 137).

FRUSTRATION

> Frustration occurs where it is established that due to a subsequent change in circumstances, the contract has become impossible to perform, or it has been deprived of its commercial purpose

The doctrine has been kept to narrow limits:

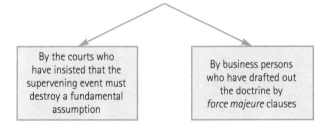

By the courts who have insisted that the supervening event must destroy a fundamental assumption

By business persons who have drafted out the doctrine by *force majeure* clauses

THE BASIS OF THE DOCTRINE AND THE TESTS

- Until the 19th century, the courts adhered to a theory of 'absolute contracts', as in *Paradine v Jane* [1647]. It was said that if the parties wished to evade liability because of some supervening event, then they should provide for this in the contract. However, in *Taylor v Caldwell* [1863], the courts relented, and held that if the contract became impossible to perform due to some extraneous cause for which neither party was responsible, then the contract would be discharged.

▶ PARADINE v JANE [1647]

Facts

Paradine sued Jane for unpaid rent. Jane argued that he had been forced off the land by a hostile army for a significant period of the lease.

Held

The obligations had not been discharged by the intervening event. The only way to avoid liability in such circumstances would be by express provision in the lease agreement.

▶ TAYLOR v CALDWELL [1863]

Facts

An agreement was entered into for the hire of a music hall to hold concerts for four days. Before the concert dates, the hall burnt down and performance was impossible

Held

Performance was impossible and both parties were excused from their obligations.

- The modern test was enunciated by Lord Simon in *National Carriers v Panalpina* [1981]: frustration arises where 'there supervenes an event (without default of either party and for which the contract makes no sufficient provision) which so significantly changes the nature (not merely the expense or onerousness) of the outstanding contractual rights and/or obligations from what the parties could reasonably have contemplated at the time of its execution that it would be unjust to hold them to the literal sense of its stipulations in the new circumstances'.

- In *Davis Contractors v Fareham UDC* [1956], Lord Radcliff stated that frustration occurs where to require performance would be to render the obligation something 'radically different' from what was undertaken by the contract.

Note – it is not the circumstances, but the nature of the obligation, which must have changed.

CIRCUMSTANCES IN WHICH FRUSTRATION MAY OCCUR

▓ The subject matter of the contract has been destroyed, or is otherwise unavailable.

In *Taylor v Caldwell* [1863], a contract to hire a music hall was held to be frustrated by the destruction of the music hall by fire (see, also, s 7 of the Sale of Goods Act 1979).

▓ But, the unavailable or destroyed object must have been intended by both parties to be the subject of the contract.

In *Blackburn Bobbin Co v Allen* [1918], the contract was for the sale of 'birch timber' which the seller intended to obtain from Finland. Held – the contract was not frustrated when it became impossible to obtain timber from Finland. The subject matter of the contract was birch timber not Finnish birch timber.

▓ Death or incapacity of a party to a contract of personal service, or a contract where the personality of one party is important.

In *Condor v The Baron Knights* [1966], a contract between a pop group and its drummer was held frustrated when the drummer became ill and was unable to fulfil the terms of the contract. A claim for unfair dismissal can also sometimes be defeated by the defence of frustration where an employee has become permanently incapacitated or imprisoned for a long period.

▓ The contract has become illegal to perform, either because of a change in the law, or the outbreak of war.

In *Avery v Bowden* [1855], a contract to supply goods to Russia was frustrated when the Crimean War broke out. It had become an illegal contract – trading with the enemy.

Note: the outbreak of war between two foreign states will not render a contract illegal, but may make it impossible to perform. In *Finelvet v Vinava Shipping Co* [1983], a contract to deliver goods to Basra did not become illegal on the outbreak of the Iraq–Iran war, but was frustrated when it became too dangerous to sail to Basra.

■ The commercial purpose of the contract has failed.

Establishing whether a contract is impossible or illegal to perform is relatively straightforward, but it is more difficult to decide whether the commercial purpose of the contract has failed.

It may happen in the following circumstances.

■ Failure of an event upon which the contract was based.

▶ KRELL v HENRY [1903]

Facts

An agreement was made for the hire of a room overlooking the proposed route of the coronation procession of King Edward VII. The King was taken ill and the coronation was postponed.

Held

The contract was frustrated. The purpose of the contract was to view the coronation, not merely to hire a room.

It has been argued that the fact that the hire of the room was a 'one off' transaction was important. The judge in the case contrasted it with the hire of a taxi to take the client to Epsom on Derby day. This would be a normal contractual transaction for the taxi driver; the cancellation of the Derby would not, therefore, frustrate the contract.

But contrast the case below.

▶ HERNE BAY STEAMBOAT CO v HUTTON [1903]

Facts

The obligations under a contract to hire a boat to see the king review the fleet were challenged when the review was cancelled.

Held

The contract was not frustrated. The fleet was still there and could be viewed – there was therefore no overall failure of the purpose of the contract.

▨ Government interference or delay.

In *Metropolitan Water Board v Dick Kerr* [1918], a contract had been formed in 1913 to build a reservoir within six years. In 1915, the government ordered the work to be stopped and the plant sold. Held – the contract was frustrated.

In *Jackson v Union Marine Insurance Co* [1874], a ship was chartered in November to proceed with all dispatch to Newport. The ship did not reach Newport until the following August. Held – the contract was frustrated since the ship was not available for the voyage for which she had been chartered.

In *The Nema* [1982], a charter party was frustrated when a long strike closed the port at which the ship was due to load, so that of the six or seven voyages contracted to be made between April and December, only two could be made.

Similar difficult problems arise in the case of contracts of employment (illness or imprisonment) and leases.

It has been suggested that, where the contract is of a fixed duration, and the unavailability of the subject matter is only temporary, the court should consider the ratio of the likely interruption to the duration of the contract.

Leases

It had long been thought that the doctrine of frustration did not apply to leases (see *Paradine v Jane* [1647] and *Cricklewood Investments v Leighton's Investments* [1945]).

▨ However, in *National Carriers v Panalpina* [1981], the HOL declared that in principle, a lease could be frustrated. In that case, a street which gave the only access to a warehouse was closed for 18 months. The lease for the warehouse was for 10 years. Held – the lease was not frustrated.

The HOL did state, however, that where there was only one purpose for the property leased, and this purpose became impossible, then the lease would be frustrated, for example, a short term holiday lease. It is still true that it will be very rare for a lease to be frustrated.

LIMITS TO THE DOCTRINE OF FRUSTRATION

'Doctrine must be kept within narrow limits'

It will not be applied:

On the grounds of inconvenience, increase in expense, loss of profit.

▶ DAVIS CONTRACTORS LTD v FAREHAM UDC [1956]

Facts

The contractors had agreed to build a council estate at a fixed price. Due to strikes, bad weather and shortages of labour and materials, there were considerable delays and the houses could only be built at a substantial loss.

Held

The contract was not frustrated.

See, also, the *Suez* cases where the courts refused to hold shipping contracts frustrated as a result of the closing of the Suez Canal unless the contracts specified a route through the canal.

Where there is an express provision in the contract covering the intervening event (that is, a *force majeure* clause).

But, a *force majeure* clause will be interpreted narrowly as in *Metropolitan Water Board v Dick Kerr & Co* [1918] where a reference to 'delays' was held to refer only to ordinary delays, and not to a delay caused by government decree.

A *force majeure* clause will not in any case be applied to cover trading with an enemy.

▨ Where the frustration is self-induced.

A contract will not be frustrated if the event making performance impossible was the voluntary action of one party. If the party concerned had a choice open to him, and chose to act so as to make performance impossible, then frustration will be self-induced and the court will refuse to treat the contract as discharged.

▶ THE *SUPERSERVANT TWO* [1990]

Facts

One of two barges owned by the defendants and used to transport oil rigs was sunk. They were therefore unable to fulfil their contract to transport an oil rig belonging to the plaintiff as their other barge (*Superservant One*) was already allocated to other contracts.

Held

The contract was not frustrated. The defendants had another barge available, but chose not to allocate it to the contract with the plaintiffs.

It is arguable that in this case there was no real choice open to the defendants. This illustrates the narrowness of the doctrine, and the advantage of a *force majeure* clause.

Where the event was foreseeable

If, by reason of special knowledge, the event was foreseeable by one party, then he cannot claim frustration.

▨ In *Amalgamated Investment and Property Co v John Walker & Sons Ltd* [1976] the possibility that a building could be listed was foreseen by the plaintiff who had enquired about the matter beforehand. A failure to obtain planning permission was also foreseeable and was a normal risk for property developers. The contract was therefore not frustrated.

THE EFFECT OF FRUSTRATION

At common law, the loss lay where it fell, that is, the date of the frustrating event was all important. Anything paid or payable before that date would have to be paid. Anything payable after that date need not be paid.

This rule could be very unfair in its operation, as in *Chandler v Webster* [1904], where the hirer had to pay all the sum due for the hire of a room to view the coronation despite the court holding the contract frustrated by the cancellation of the coronation.

In the *Fibrosa* case [1943], the HOL did move away from this rule and held that where there was a total failure of consideration, then any money paid or payable in advance would have to be returned.

This rule, however, would only apply in the event of a total failure of consideration, and could itself in any case cause hardship if the other party had expended a considerable amount of money in connection with the contract.

The Law Reform (Frustrated Contracts) Act 1943 was therefore passed to remedy these deficiencies. It provided:

> s 1(2) – all sums paid or payable before the frustrating event shall be recoverable or cease to be payable, but the court has a discretionary power to allow the payee to set off against the sum so paid expenses he has incurred before the frustrating event.

> s 1(3) – where one party has obtained a valuable benefit, before the time of discharge, the other party may recover from him such sums as the court considers just.

Note – these two sections are to be applied independently. The expenses in s 1(2) can only be recovered from 'sums paid or payable before the frustrating event'. Set-off will be granted only where it is just and equitable having regard to all the circumstances of the case.

▶ GAMERCO SA v ICM/FAIR WARNING (AGENCY) LTD [1995]

Facts

The plaintiffs agreed to promote a rock concert to be performed by Guns 'N' Roses. The contract was frustrated at a time when the plaintiffs had paid $412,000 to the defendants in advance, and incurred $400,000 worth of expenditure. The defendants had also incurred preparatory expenditure, but it was relatively small and unsubstantiated.

Set-off was not exercised in the defendant's favour, and the plaintiffs recovered their entire $412,000 advance payment.

Section 1(3) was applied in *BP Exploration v Hunt* [1982] where it was held that the court must:

▨ identify and value the 'benefit obtained';

▨ assess the 'just sum' which it is proper to award.

The court also stated that:

▨ the section was designed to prevent unjust enrichment, not to apportion the loss, or to place the parties in the position they would be in had the contract been performed, or to restore them to their pre-contract position;

▨ in assessing the valuable benefit, the section required reference to the end benefit received by a party, not the cost of performance. In assessing the end benefit, the effect of the frustrating event had to be taken into account;

▨ the cost of performance can be taken into account in assessing the just sum;

▶ BP EXPLORATION v HUNT [1982]

Facts
BP were to do the exploration and provide the necessary finance on an oil concession owned by Mr Hunt in Libya. They were also to provide certain 'farm-in' payments in cash and oil. In return, they were to get a half-share in the concession and 5% of their expenditure in reimbursement oil. A large field was discovered, the oil began to flow; then, in 1971, the Libyan Government nationalised the field.

> **Held**
>
> The valuable benefit to Hunt was the net amount of oil received plus the compensation payable by the Libyan Government which amounted to £85,000,000.

■ the just sum would cover the work done by BP less the value of the reimbursement oil already received. This was assessed at £34,000,000. As the valuable benefit exceeded the just sum, BP recovered their expenses in full. The position would have been very different, however, if the field had been nationalised at an earlier stage and no compensation had been paid.

The Law Reform (Frustrated Contracts) Act 1943 does not apply to:

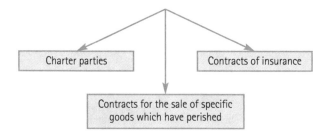

Charter parties

Contracts of insurance

Contracts for the sale of specific goods which have perished

You should now be confident that you would be able to tick all of the boxes on the checklist at the beginning of this chapter. To check your knowledge of Discharge why not visit the companion website and take the Multiple Choice Question test. Check your understanding of the terms and vocabulary used in this chapter with the flashcard glossary.

9

Remedies for breach of contract and restitution

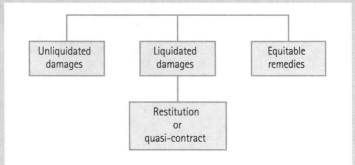

UNLIQUIDATED DAMAGES

Damages assessed by the court

The purpose of unliquidated damages is to compensate the claimant for the loss he has suffered as a result of a breach

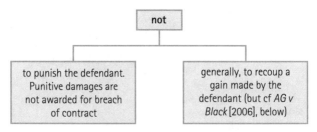

not

to punish the defendant. Punitive damages are not awarded for breach of contract

generally, to recoup a gain made by the defendant (but cf *AG v Black* [2006], below)

If no loss has been suffered, then nominal damages only will be awarded.

- In *Surrey CC v Bredero Homes* [1993], the court refused to award damages against a defendant who had not complied with planning permission as there was no loss to the council.

- However, in *Chaplin v Hicks* [1911], damages were awarded for the loss of a chance to win a competition, although there was no certainty that the plaintiff would have won.

METHODS OF COMPENSATING THE CLAIMANT

Expectation, that is, loss of bargain is the traditional basis for assessing damages in contract. It aims to put the claimant in the same position, as far as money can do it, as if the contract had been performed	*Reliance*, that is, out of pocket or wasted expenditure. This is the normal way of assessing damages in tort, but can be used in contract, as illustrated below

Reliance damages rather than expectation damages may be appropriate where the benefits which would have been obtained by successful performance are difficult to assess, as in:

- *McRae v Commonwealth Disposals Commission* [1951], where the plaintiff recovered the expenses incurred in searching for a wreck which did not exist.

- *Anglia Television v Reed* [1972], where the leading actor in a film project withdrew at the last moment. The plaintiffs were able to recover all their wasted expenditure on the programme, including even that incurred before the contract had been signed.

- But, cf *Regalian Properties v London Dockland Development* [1995] where expenses incurred while negotiations were expressly 'subject to contract' were not recoverable.

It has been held that a claimant may freely choose between expectation and reliance damages, unless the difficulty in identifying profits is because he has made a 'bad bargain'.

- In *C and P Haulage v Middleton* [1983], the plaintiff hired a garage for six months on the basis that any improvements would become the property of the landlord. He was ejected in breach of contract, and sued for the cost of the improvements. Held – expenditure would have been wasted even if the contract had been performed.

▓ It is for the defendant to prove that the claimant had made a bad bargain, as in *CCC Films v Impact Quadrant Films* [1985] where the defendant failed to prove that the plaintiff would not have made a profit from distributing the films had they been delivered in accordance with the contract.

▓ In normal circumstances, the claimant will ask for damages on an expectation basis, as this is more profitable for him.

RESTITUTIONARY MEASURE

In *Attorney General v Blake* [2000], the HOL for the first time recognised that in some circumstances a 'restitutionary' measure of damages, requiring the defendant to pay over the profit made as a result of the breach of contract, may be appropriate. The case was an unusual one, involving a book published by a member of the security services who had spied for Russia. The HOL regarded the defendant as having been under something 'akin to a fiduciary obligation'. Subsequent cases suggest that the principle is narrow in scope.

Two cases illustrate the courts' reluctance to extend the principle in *Blake* to other factual scenarios.

▶ 'THE SINE NOMINEE' [2002]

Facts

The owners of a ship under a charter contract failed to make the ship available to the charterers. The charterers sought to recover the profits the owners had made through alternative use of the ship.

Held

The arbitrators stated that an award of wrongful profits would not generally be available where both parties were dealing with a marketable commodity, but that damages based on the reliance interest (ie the difference between the contract price and the market price) would effectively achieve this (although this assumes that the cost of finding an alternative ship, and the profits available from hiring the ship out elsewhere, were the same).

> ▶ EXPERIENCE HENDRIX v PPX ENTERPRISES INC [2003]
>
> **Facts**
> The defendants breached the terms of a settlement by granting licences to Jimi Hendrix recordings when they were not entitled to do so. The claimants sought to recover the profits.
>
> **Held**
> COA awarded a 'reasonable sum', to account for the sum which the Jimi Hendrix estate might reasonably have demanded as payment for the additional licensing rights.

The approach of the COA in the latter case has the advantage of flexibility, but essentially involves the court in creating a collateral contract, which is arguably undesirable.

CONTRIBUTORY NEGLIGENCE
This is only relevant where the liability in contract is identical with the liability in tort, that is, the breach is of a contractual duty to take care (*Barclays Bank v Fairclough Building* [1994]).

QUANTIFICATION OF DAMAGE
Where 'loss of bargain' damages are claimed, there are two possible methods of quantification.

The court will normally adopt the most appropriate (*Ruxley Electronics and Construction v Forsyth* [1995]).

PRIMA FACIE RULES

Sale of goods – difference in value

Failure to repair (lease) – difference in value

Building contracts – cost of cure

Failure to deliver goods

The Sale of Goods Act 1979 states that damages will represent the difference between the contract price and the market price

■ In *Williams Bros v Agius* [1914], the profit that would have been earned on a resale was ignored; damages represented the difference between the contract price and the market price (which was higher than the resale price).

Failure to accept delivery and pay

The Sale of Goods Act 1979 states that damages will again represent the difference between the contract price and the market price

■ If the seller is a dealer in mass produced goods, then the damage to him will be the loss of profit on one transaction. The claimant had sold one item less than he otherwise would have during the year (*Thomson v Robinson* [1955]).

■ However, if the mass produced item is in short supply and the number of sales is governed by supply not by demand, then there is no loss of profit and damages would not be awarded (*Charter v Sullivan* [1957]).

■ The damages revert to the difference between the contract price and market price in the case of second hand goods even if the seller is a dealer (*Lazenby Garages v Wright* [1976]).

LIMITATIONS ON PRINCIPLE OF EXPECTATION

Although the stated aim of the expectation basis of assessing damages is to put the claimant in the position he would have been in had the contract been performed, a number of rules militate against this result.

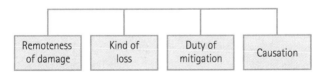

REMOTENESS OF DAMAGE

> Damages cannot be recovered for losses that are too remote. The losses must be 'within the reasonable contemplation' of the parties

The two situations in which the requirements of remoteness will be satisfied are laid down in the case of *Hadley v Baxendale* [1854]. These are referred to as the two limbs of remoteness of damage.

▶ HADLEY v BAXENDALE [1854]

Facts

A mill was closed because of the delay of a carrier in returning a mill shaft. The mill owner sued for loss of profit.

Held

The court held that the following damages were recoverable:
● those arising naturally out of the breach;
● those which because of special knowledge would have been within the contemplation of the parties.

In essence, *Hadley v Baxendale* defines the type of damage that can be compensated.

▨ In *Victoria Laundry v Newman Industries* [1949], the rule was restated, as being knowledge-based.

▶ VICTORIA LAUNDRY v NEWMAN INDUSTRIES [1949]

Facts

The defendants delayed the delivery of a boiler by five months. The laundry sued for loss of normal profits, and loss of profit from a specially lucrative dyeing contract.

Held

The laundry was able to recover damages for normal loss of profit but not for the lucrative dyeing contract as the defendants were not aware of the special contract when they entered into the agreement.

Damages were said to be recoverable for losses which were within the reasonable contemplation of the parties at the time of the contract either from:

● imputed knowledge; or

● actual knowledge.

▪ In *The Heron II* [1969], the HOL confirmed that a higher degree of foreseeability is required in contract than in tort. For a loss not to be too remote, there must be:

● 'a real danger';

● 'a serious possibility'; of the loss occurring

or the loss must be:

● 'not unlikely';

● 'liable to result'.

The difference between the tests of remoteness in contract and tort has been criticised, but justified on the ground that a contracting party can protect himself against unusual risks in the contract itself.

Application of remoteness rules

▪ Imputed knowledge.

Hadley v Baxendale [1854]

Victoria Laundry v Newman Industries [1949]

The Heron II [1967]

▨ Actual knowledge.

Defendant's knowledge of special circumstances must be precise. This encourages contracting parties to disclose clearly any likely exceptional losses in advance.

In *Simpson v L & NWR* [1876], the defendant was liable for loss caused to the plaintiff by delivering goods to Newcastle Show Ground the day after the show had finished.

Where an unusual activity of the claimant has increased the loss caused by the defendant's breach, the defendant will be liable only if he had knowledge of that activity. In *Balfour Beatty Construction (Scotland) Ltd v Scottish Power Plc* [1994], the interruption of the supply of electricity rendered the work undertaken on a construction project worthless. The electricity supplier had been unaware of the special requirements of the process, and was not liable for all of the losses.

Note: the test of remoteness determines entitlement, not quantum

---

▨ In *Wroth v Tyler* [1974], the defendant was liable for the full difference between the contract price and the market price, although the rise in the market price was exceptional and unforeseeable.

▨ In *Parsons (Livestock) Ltd v Uttley Ingham Co Ltd* [1978], the defendants who had supplied inadequately ventilated hoppers for pig food were held liable for the loss of the plaintiff's pigs, even though the disease from which they died was not foreseeable. It was enough that they could have contemplated any illness of the pigs.

▨ The extent of the risk that must be contemplated is not always easy to ascertain. The difficulty with current precedent is that there is a lack of clarity as to how likely or usual a loss must be for it to be recoverable.

The HOL' decision in *Jackson v Royal Bank of Scotland plc* [2005] has partially clarified matters.

▶ JACKSON v ROYAL BANK OF SCOTLAND PLC [2005]

Facts

The claimants were an import company with one major customer (X). The bank, in breach of its contractual duty of confidentiality, revealed the extent of the mark-up on the imported goods to X, whereupon X withdrew its business from the claimants. The claimants claimed damages in respect of their future profits from their supply contract with X.

Held

The trial judge awarded damages in respect of four years' trading, on a reducing basis. COA overturned this award, and awarded damages in respect of only one year's trading, on the basis that the correct cut-off period for the bank's liability was the end of such period as would have been within their reasonable contemplation at the time of the breach. The HOL reverted to the trial judge's award.

In making its award the HOL made the following points:

- The date of the **contract**, not the date of the breach, is the relevant date for the purpose of *Hadley v Baxendale*.

- Once the claimants had shown that damage of the kind suffered was within the reasonable contemplation of the bank at the time of making the contract, the only limitation on quantum was the point at which the future profits were too speculative to be recoverable.

- The trial judge's estimate of four years as the cut-off point was as good an estimate as any.

This approach confirms that taken in *Parsons v Uttley*, and *Wroth v Tyler*, and extends the principle to future profits.

In the recent HOL decision of *Transfield Shipping Inc v Mercator Shipping Inc* [2008], the late return of a charter by the defendants resulted in a delay in a contract for the charter between the owners and a third party. The owners sued the defendant for their full losses from the third party contract, which had been agreed at a lucrative price when hire prices were higher. The majority view of the HOL was that it was highly unlikely that the extreme price fluctuations could have been foreseen by the defendant and the volatility of the market would not have been contemplated by the parties when forming the contract. Thus they were entitled to be paid for the overrun to market rate only.

Types of loss recognised

Pecuniary loss

This is the normal ground for the award of damages for breach of contract.

Non-pecuniary loss

However, damages for non-pecuniary loss will be awarded in specific cases, for example:

- Pain and suffering consequent on physical injury.

- Physical inconvenience.

    In *Watts v Morrow* [1991], damages were awarded to cover the inconvenience of living in a house whilst it was being repaired.

- Damage to commercial reputation.

    In *Gibbons v Westminster Bank* [1939], damages were awarded to cover the losses caused by the wrongful referring of a cheque.

    Cf *Malik v BCCI* [1997] where the HOL held that compensation was payable for the stigma of having worked for an organisation which had been run corruptly.

- Distress to claimant.

    Traditionally, damages for injured feelings were not awarded for breach of contract: *Addis v Gramophone Co* [1909]. This general principle has been confirmed by the HOL in *Johnson v Unisys Ltd* [2001].

    However, some limited exceptions to this rule have been recognised.

- Damages for disappointment were awarded against a holiday company in *Jarvis v Swan Tours* [1973] where the holiday was not as described.

■ In *Hayes v Dodd* [1990], the COA confirmed that damages for distress are not recoverable in normal commercial contracts, but could be recovered in contracts:

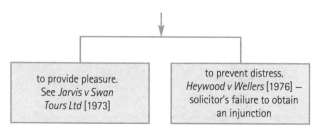

to provide pleasure. See *Jarvis v Swan Tours Ltd* [1973]

to prevent distress. *Heywood v Wellers* [1976] — solicitor's failure to obtain an injunction

In *Eastwood v Magnox Electric plc* [2004], a further exception to the *Unisys* rule was discussed. An employee can recover damages for distress caused by an employer's failure to act fairly in implementing a dismissal procedure, although not for the manner of the dismissal itself.

It has been suggested that damages for distress are particularly appropriate in 'consumer contracts'.

According to the HOL, it is sufficient if one of the major objects of the contract is to provide pleasure or to relieve anxiety. Thus, in *Farley v Skinner* [2001], the claimant recovered damages from a surveyor for failure to provide peace of mind when the surveyor failed to advise him that a house which he went on to purchase was on the flight path from Gatwick Airport.

The definition of such contracts is wide; for example, a contract of retainer with a solicitor to prevent a child being abducted from the UK was held to be included in this category, in *Hamilton Jones v David & Snape* (a firm) [2004].

The duty of mitigation

> The claimant has a duty to take reasonable steps to mitigate his loss

In *Payzu v Saunders* [1919], the plaintiff had refused the offer of goods at below market price. In *Brace v Calder* [1895], an employee dismissed by a partnership turned down an offer of similar employment by one of the partners. In both cases, the plaintiff was penalised for his failure to mitigate.

▧ He need not, however, take 'unreasonable' steps in mitigation.

In *Pilkington v Wood* [1953], it was stated that the plaintiff did not need to embark on hazardous legal action in mitigation of his loss. He should not take unreasonable steps which would increase losses.

▧ The claimant cannot recover damages for losses he has avoided.

In *British Westinghouse v Underground Electric Railways Co* [1912], the plaintiff replaced a defective turbine with a new turbine which was so much more efficient that the savings exceeded the losses on the defective turbine. Held – no loss – no damages.

▧ Note – the duty to mitigate does not arise until there has been an actual breach of contract, or an anticipatory breach has been accepted by the other party (see *White and Carter v McGregor*).

Causation (losses which the defendant did not cause)

> The breach must have caused the loss as well as having preceded the loss

▧ The action of a third party may break the chain of causation if it is not foreseeable.

In *Lambert v Lewis* [1981], a farmer continued to use a coupling even though he knew it was broken. Held – the farmer was responsible for losses caused by the failure of the coupling; the manufacturer could not have foreseen that he would continue to use it.

▧ However, where the action is foreseeable, the chain of causation will not be broken.

In *Stansbie v Troman* [1948], a painter who, in breach of contract, had left a door unlocked, was held liable for goods taken by thieves, since this was the kind of loss he had undertaken to guard against by locking the doors.

Where events have occurred after a breach and they affect the value of the loss, the courts will consider the loss at the time of assessment.

> ## GOLDEN STRAIT CORP. V NIPPON YUSEN KUBISHIKA KAISHA (THE GOLDEN VICTORY) [2007]

A ship was returned four years earlier than due (2001), in breach of contract.

Facts

The contract had contained a clause which allowed termination in the event of war. A war broke out 15 months after the breach of contract.

Held

HOL held that the shipowner's losses could only be recovered for the 15 months period, up until the time that the contract would have been legitimately terminated when war broke out.

LIQUIDATED DAMAGES

Damages set by the parties themselves

The parties may stipulate that a certain sum must be paid on a breach of contract

If the sum represents a genuine pre-estimate, then it will be enforced by the court as liquidated damages

If the sum is not genuine, but is an attempt to frighten the other party into performing, then it is a penalty and unenforceable

The following guidelines for distinguishing between the two were suggested in *Dunlop Pneumatic Tyre Ltd v New Garage and Motor Co* [1915]:

- a penalty – if the sum is extravagant and unconscionable;

- a penalty – if a larger sum is payable on the failure to pay a smaller sum;

- a penalty – if the same sum is payable on major and minor breaches;

- it is no obstacle to the sum being liquidated damages that a precise pre-estimate is almost impossible.

> Penalty clauses will not be enforced by the court. Instead, the court will award unliquidated damages

The rule against penalties does not apply to:

- Acceleration clauses.

  Here, the whole of a debt becomes payable immediately if certain conditions are not observed.

- Deposits.

  Money paid otherwise than on a breach of contract.

  Alder v Moore [1961]

  Bridge v Campbell Discount Co Ltd [1962]

- Clauses declaring a term to be a condition.

  Lombard North Central v Butterworth [1987]

EQUITABLE REMEDIES

| Specific performance | Injunctions |

SPECIFIC PERFORMANCE

Traditionally, specific performance will only be awarded where damages are not an adequate remedy, that is:

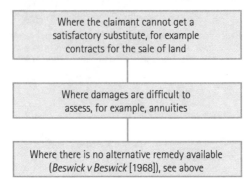

Where the claimant cannot get a
satisfactory substitute, for example
contracts for the sale of land

Where damages are difficult to
assess, for example, annuities

Where there is no alternative remedy available
(*Beswick v Beswick* [1968]), see above

The following will be taken into account:

- Mutuality. Negative – a minor cannot get it because it is not available against a minor. Positive – a vendor of land may obtain it although damages would be an adequate remedy, because it is also available to a purchaser of land.

- Supervision. The need for constant supervision prevented the appointment of a resident porter being ordered in *Ryan v Mutual Tontine Association* [1893] but not in *Posner v Scott Lewis* [1986], where the terms of the contract were sufficiently precise.

- Impossibility – *Watts v Spence* [1976] – land belonged to a third party.

- Hardship – *Patel v Ali* [1984] – defendant would lose the help of supportive neighbours.

- Conduct of the claimant – *Shell (UK) Ltd v Lostock Garages* [1977] – Shell's behaviour was unreasonable.

- Vagueness – *Tito v Waddell* [1977] – see above.

- Mistake – *Webster v Cecil* [1861] – see above.

SPECIAL PROBLEMS

- Contracts of personal service.

These are considered to involve personal relationships and are therefore not thought suitable for an order of specific performance.

However, such orders were exceptionally made in *Hill v CA Parsons Ltd* [1972] and *Irani v Southampton AHA* [1985].

- Building contracts.

  The courts are reluctant to enforce building contracts on the grounds that damages are generally an adequate remedy; the terms are often vague; there are difficulties with supervision.

  But, it was held in *Wolverhampton Corpn v Emmons* [1901] that, provided the terms were clear, the problem of supervision would not be an absolute barrier.

INJUNCTIONS

> These are orders directing the defendant not to do a certain act

TYPES OF INJUNCTION

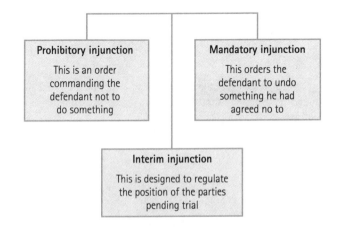

Prohibitory injunction	Mandatory injunction
This is an order commanding the defendant not to do something	This orders the defendant to undo something he had agreed no to

Interim injunction

This is designed to regulate the position of the parties pending trial

Injunctions are also discretionary remedies and are subject to the similar constraints to orders of specific performance. However, an injunction will be granted to enforce a negative stipulation in a contract of employment, as long as this is not an indirect way of enforcing the contract.

▩ *Warner Bros Pictures Inc v Nelson* [1937];

▩ cf *Page One Records v Britton* [1968].

▶ WARNER BROS PICTURES INC v NELSON [1937]

Facts

The actress Bette Davis was contracted to WB exclusively for a one year period, with an option to extend the period. During the period of contract she agreed to act for a competitor of WB.

Held

The court granted an injunction which prevented her from working for the competitor.

▶ PAGE ONE RECORDS v BRITTON [1968]

Facts

The 1960s pop group, 'The Troggs' were prevented indefinitely by their contract from appointing another person to work as their manager. The group were dissatisfied with their current manager and appointed another.

Held

The courts refused to grant an injunction as it would prevent the group from working as musicians or would tie them to a personal contract against their wishes.

A COMPARISON OF THE REMEDIES FOR MISREPRESENTATION AND FOR BREACH OF CONTRACT

Setting aside contracts

	Termination or rescission for breach
Breach	Available only for breaches of conditions, fundamental breaches of innominate terms and repudiations
	Contract discharged from time of breach; discharge not retrospective. Innocent party can also sue for damages (see Chapter 8)
	Rescission
Misrep	Available for all misrepresentations, but at discretion of court, and subject to certain bars. Contract cancelled prospectively and retrospectively; parties returned to the position they were in before the contract was entered into (see Chapter 5)
	Damages
Breach	Damages available as of right. Normally assessed on expectation basis. Losses must be within the contemplation of the parties. See above
Misrep	Damages available in tort of deceit; negligent statements; and under s 2(1) of the 1967 Act
	Damages assessed on reliance basis. All losses flowing directly from misrepresentation will be covered, whether or not foreseeable, in actions in deceit, and under s 2(1) of the 1967 Act (*Royscot v Rogerson* (1991)). Losses must be foreseeable in the tort of negligence. No right to damages for innocent misrepresentation but may be awarded in lieu of rescission at the discretion of the court
	Exclusion clauses
Breach	See ss 3, 6, 7 of UCTA
Misrep	All clauses must be reasonable

RESTITUTION OR QUASI-CONTRACT (BASED ON UNJUST ENRICHMENT)

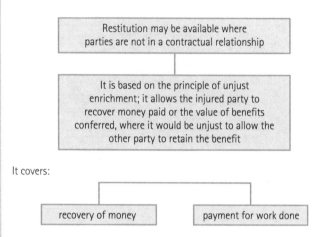

Restitution may be available where
parties are not in a contractual relationship

It is based on the principle of unjust
enrichment; it allows the injured party to
recover money paid or the value of benefits
conferred, where it would be unjust to allow the
other party to retain the benefit

It covers:

| recovery of money | payment for work done |

MONEY MAY BE RECOVERED

▨ Where there is a total failure of consideration (see *Fibrosa* case (frustration)).

In *Rowland v Divall* [1923], the plaintiff had bought a car which turned out to be stolen property, and which was recovered by the owner. Despite the fact that the plaintiff had had the use of the car for a considerable time, and it had fallen in value during this time, the plaintiff was able to recover the full purchase price of the car from the defendant. There had been a total failure of consideration.

▨ Money paid under a mistake of fact is recoverable, provided the mistake is as to a fact which, if true, would have legally or morally obliged the claimant to pay the money, or is sufficiently serious to require payment (see example below).

| Mistaken payments under insurance policies | Mistaken payments into a bank account |

In *Kleinwort Benson Ltd v Lincoln City Council* [1998], the HOL held that in certain circumstances money paid under a mistake of law could also be recovered, if it would be unjust to allow the recipient to retain the money. (See, also, *Nurdin and Peacock plc v DB Ramsden & Co Ltd* [1999].)

▨ Money paid under a void contract: see below:

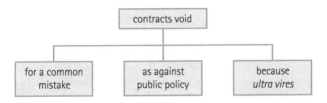

▶ WESTDEUTSCHE LANDESBANK v ISLINGTON LBC [1994]

Facts

The council had entered into a rate swapping arrangement with the bank, under which the bank had paid £2,500,000 to the council in advance. The council had paid approximately £1,200,000 to the bank by instalment, and argued that since there was not a total failure of consideration, it should not have to pay the bank the remaining £1,300,000.

Held

COA held that the principle upon which money must be repaid under a void contract is different from that on a total failure of consideration. Recovery of money under a void contract is allowed if there is no legal basis for such a payment.

▨ Note – money paid under a contract which is void for illegality cannot be recovered, unless the action can be framed without relying on the contract.

Parkinson v Royal College of Ambulance [1925]

Bowmakers v Barnet Instruments [1945]

Tinsley v Milligan [1993]

Note – recovery under these heads will not be possible if:

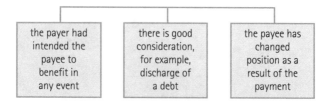

| the payer had intended the payee to benefit in any event | there is good consideration, for example, discharge of a debt | the payee has changed position as a result of the payment |

In *Lipkin Gorman v Karpnale Ltd* [1992], a partner in a firm of solicitors regularly gambled at a casino run by the defendants. In order to finance his gambling, he had drawn cheques on client accounts where he was the sole signatory. He had spent at least £154,000 of this money at the defendants' casino, and the plaintiff sued for the return of the money, as it had been received under a contract which was void (declared void by statute). Held – where the true owner of stolen money sought to recover it from an innocent third party, the recipient was under an obligation to return it where he had given no consideration for it, unless he could show that he had altered his position in good faith. In this case, the plaintiff was able to recover the £154,000 less the winnings paid to the partner. The casino had altered their position on each gamble in that they had become vulnerable to a loss.

However, in *South Tyneside Metropolitan Borough Council v Svenska International* [1994], the HOL allowed the council to recover approximately £200,000 it had paid to a bank under a rate swap agreement which had been declared *ultra vires* and void. The court rejected the bank's claim that it had changed its position in that it had entered into financial arrangements with other organisations in order to hedge its losses.

Money paid to a third party for the benefit of the defendant provided the claimant was not acting as a volunteer (for example, a mother paying off a son's debt), but was acting under some constraint.

In *Macclesfield Corpn v Great Central Railway* [1911], the plaintiffs carried out repairs to a bridge which the defendants were legally obliged (but had refused) to maintain. They were regarded as purely volunteers, and could not therefore recover the money. However, in *Exall v Partridge* [1799], the plaintiff paid off arrears of rent owed by the defendant in order to avoid seizure of the plaintiff's carriage which was kept on the defendant's premises. The plaintiff was acting under a constraint, and could therefore recover the money.

PAYMENT FOR WORK DONE

Here, the claimant is seeking compensation on a *quantum meruit* basis (cf s 1(3) of the Law Reform (Frustrated Contracts) Act 1943)

▦ Where the claimant has prevented performance of the contract (see *Planché v Colburn* [1831]).

▦ Where work has been carried out under a void contract.

In *Craven Ellis v Canons Ltd* [1936], the plaintiff had carried out a great deal of work on behalf of a company on the understanding that he had been appointed managing director. It was later discovered that he had not properly been appointed managing director. The court held that he should be paid on a *quantum meruit* basis for the work he had done.

▦ Where agreement has not been reached, and:

● the work was requested by the defendants. In *William Lacey v Davis* [1957], the plaintiffs had submitted the lowest tender for a building contract, and had been led to believe that they would be awarded it. At the defendants' request, they then prepared various plans and estimates. The defendants then decided not to proceed. The court ordered the defendants to pay a reasonable sum on a *quantum meruit* basis for the work that had been done; or

● the work had been freely accepted. In *British Steel Corpn v Cleveland Bridge Engineering Co* [1984], a letter of intent was issued by the defendants, indicating that they intended to enter into a contract with the plaintiffs for the construction and delivery of cast-steel 'nodes'. However, it proved impossible to reach agreement on a number of major items. Despite this, a number of nodes were eventually constructed, and accepted by the defendants. It was held by the court that the defendants should pay for the nodes they had accepted.

You should now be confident that you would be able to tick all of the boxes on the checklist at the beginning of this chapter. To check your knowledge of Remedies for breach of contract and restitution why not visit the companion website and take the Multiple Choice Question test. Check your understanding of the terms and vocabulary used in this chapter with the flashcard glossary.

10

Privity of contract

INTRODUCTION

The traditional approach to the doctrine of privity is that:

Only a party to a contract can sue on a contract	Only a party to a contract can be sued on a contract
In *Tweddle v Atkinson* [1861], the plaintiff had married Mr Guy's daughter. The plaintiff's father and Mr Guy had agreed together that they would each pay a sum of money to the plaintiff. Mr Guy died before the money was paid, and the plaintiff sued his executors. The action was dismissed – the plaintiff was not a party to the contract, which was made between the two fathers. See also, *Beswick v Beswick* [1968]	In *Dunlop v Selfridge* [1915], Dew & Co, at the instigation of Dunlop, had placed a minimum resale price in their contract with Selfridge. Held– Dunlop could not sue Selfridge for breach of contract; they were not parties to the contract, nor had they given consideration to Selfridge

Privity of contract is closely associated with the rule that consideration must move from the promisee. See *Dunlop v Selfridge* (above).

MATTERS RELEVANT TO THE DOCTRINE OF PRIVITY

One part of the traditional approach, that is, that relating to conferring benefits, has recently been significantly changed by legislation, which is discussed below. In addition, there are a number of situations which fall outside the scope of the doctrine.

MATTERS OUTSIDE THE DOCTRINE

It has been argued that it is only because English law has declared many transactions not to be subject to the doctrine of privity that the doctrine itself has survived so long.

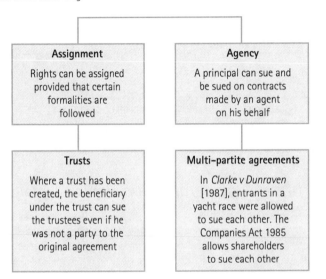

Assignment

Rights can be assigned provided that certain formalities are followed

Agency

A principal can sue and be sued on contracts made by an agent on his behalf

Trusts

Where a trust has been created, the beneficiary under the trust can sue the trustees even if he was not a party to the original agreement

Multi-partite agreements

In *Clarke v Dunraven* [1987], entrants in a yacht race were allowed to sue each other. The Companies Act 1985 allows shareholders to sue each other

Collateral contracts

In limited cases, the court will find a separate (collateral) contract between the promisor and the third party (*Shanklin Pier v Detel Products* [1951])

Land law recognises a number of exceptions.

STATUTORY EXCEPTIONS

- Price maintenance agreements
- Various insurance contracts
- Law of Property Act 1925, s 56
- Negotiable instruments

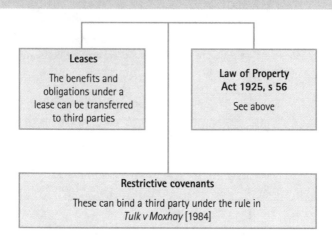

Leases

The benefits and obligations under a lease can be transferred to third parties

Law of Property Act 1925, s 56

See above

Restrictive covenants

These can bind a third party under the rule in *Tulk v Moxhay* [1984]

CONFERRING BENEFITS ON A THIRD PARTY

STATUTORY INTERVENTION

The common law rule preventing a third party from enforcing a contract was much criticised, and has now been reformed by legislation, that is, the Contracts (Rights of Third Parties) Act 1999, based on recommendations from the Law Commission.

Main effect

A third party will be able to enforce a contractual provision purporting to confer a benefit on him or her, if both of two conditions are satisfied (s 1):

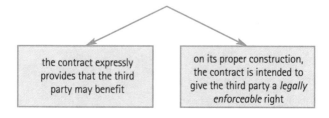

the contract expressly provides that the third party may benefit

on its proper construction, the contract is intended to give the third party a *legally enforceable* right

RIGHT TO VARY THE CONTRACT

Unless they have provided otherwise, the contracting parties will lose the right to vary or cancel the provision benefiting the third party if (s 2):

- the third party has communicated his assent; or

- the third party has relied on the term, and the promisor is aware of this; or

- the third party has relied on the term and the promisor could be reasonably expected to have foreseen this.

Defences

The promisor can raise against the third party any defences that could have been raised against the promisee (for example, misrepresentation, duress) (s 3).

The promisor can also rely on defences, set-offs or counterclaims arising from prior dealings with the third party.

Exceptions

There cannot be double liability, that is, as against the promisee and the third party (s 5).

Some contracts are excluded from the Act (s 6):

- contracts on a bill of exchange or promissory note;

- terms of a contract of employment, as against an employee;

- contracts for the carriage of goods by sea or, if subject to an international transport convention, by road, rail or air.

The exception for carriage of goods by sea does not apply to reliance on an exclusion clause (as in *The Eurymedon* [1975], for example).

Note, also, that the main contracting parties are in control – they can decide that the provisions of the new Act should not apply, and there will be nothing that the third party can do about it.

The Act does not affect the other part of the privity doctrine – relating to the imposition of obligations on third parties – which remains governed by the common law.

THE COMMON LAW APPROACH

The common law developed a number of devices to allow a third party to receive the benefit of contract by:

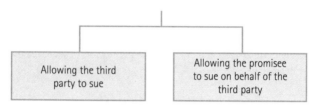

| Allowing the third party to sue | Allowing the promisee to sue on behalf of the third party |

These devices will be of much less importance now that the Contracts (Rights of Third Parties) Act 1999 is in force. They may still be used, however, particularly in situations where, for one reason or another, the 1999 Act does not apply.

Attempts to allow the third party to sue

▨ Attempts to extend the use of 'trusts'.

● In *Walford's* case [1919], under a charter party, the ship owner promised the charterer to pay a broker a commission. Held – the charterer was trustee of this promise for the broker, who could thus enforce it against the ship owner.

● However, in *Re Schebsman* [1944], a contract between Schebsman and X Ltd, that, in certain circumstances, his wife and daughter should be paid a lump sum, was held not to create a trust.

The trust as a device to outflank privity was limited by the courts, presumably because of concern that the irrevocable nature of the trust may prevent the contracting parties from changing their minds. The courts no longer go out of their way to find that the parties intended to create a trust.

▨ Lord Denning launched a campaign against privity, and argued that s 56 of the Law of Property Act 1925 intended to destroy the doctrine altogether. This was finally rejected by the HOL in *Beswick v Beswick* [1968]; they acknowledged that the wording was wide enough to support Lord Denning's view, but insisted, nevertheless, that it must be restricted to contracts concerning land as the purpose of the Act was to consolidate the law relating to real property.

▨ Agency.

Agency has been used to allow a third party to take advantage of an exclusion clause in a contract to which he was not a party.

● The HOL refused to allow stevedores to rely on an exclusion clause in a contract between the carriers and the cargo owner in *Scruttons v Midland Silicones* [1962] on the basis that only a party to the contract could claim the benefit of the contract.

● However, in *The Eurymedon* [1975], the Privy Council, on similar facts, held that the carriers had negotiated a second contract (a collateral contract) as agents of the stevedores, and the stevedores could claim the benefit of the exclusion clause in this contract.

● But, in *Southern Water Authority v Carey* [1985], sub-contractors sought to rely on a limitation of liability clause in a main contract. Held – they must have specific authority to negotiate on behalf of a third party, before this device could work.

● In *Norwich City Council v Harvey* [1989], instead of using an exclusion clause, the contract placed the risk of loss or damage by fire on the owner, and this protected both main contractor and sub-contractor.

Attempts to allow the promisee to enforce the contract on behalf of the third party

▨ Specific performance.

▶ BESWICK v BESWICK [1968]

Facts

Peter Beswick had transferred his business to his nephew, in return for his nephew's promise to pay his uncle a pension and, after his death, an annuity to his widow. The nephew paid his uncle the pension, but only one payment of the annuity was made.

> **Held**
>
> The widow, as administratrix of her husband's estate, was successful in her claim for specific performance of the contract against her nephew to pay the annuity, although the HOL implied that she would not have succeeded if she had been suing in her own right.

▨ Injunction.

Similarly, an injunction may be awarded to restrain a breach of a negative promise on a suit brought by the promisee, for example, A promised B not to compete with C, or by a stay of proceedings.

In *Snelling v Snelling Ltd* [1973], three brothers lent money to a family company, and agreed not to reclaim the money for a certain period. A stay of proceedings was granted to one of the brothers to stop another brother from breaking his promise and suing the company for the return of his money.

▨ Damages.

Damages to cover the disappointment of a third party were sanctioned by Lord Denning in *Jackson v Horizon Holidays Ltd* [1975] where the plaintiff entered into a contract with a holiday firm for a holiday for his family and himself in Ceylon. The holiday was a disaster. The plaintiff recovered damages for £500 for 'mental stress'. On appeal, the court confirmed the amount, on the ground that witnessing the distress of his family had increased the plaintiff's own distress. Lord Denning, however, stated that the sum was excessive for the plaintiff's own distress, but upheld the award on the ground that the plaintiff had made the contract on behalf of himself and of his wife and children, and that he could recover in respect of their loss as well as his own.

This statement by Lord Denning was disapproved by the HOL in *Woodar Investment Development Ltd v Wimpey Construction (UK) Ltd* [1980]. They stated that damages should not generally be recovered on behalf of a third party.

Lord Wilberforce, however, did suggest that there was a special category of contracts which called for special treatment. That is, where one party contracted for a benefit to be shared equally between a group, for example, family holidays, ordering meals in restaurants for a party, hiring taxis for a group. The decision in *Jackson* could, therefore, be supported on this ground. A further exception was identified by the HOL in *Linden Gardens Trust v Lenesta Sludge Disposals Ltd* [1993], where in a construction contract the original property owner may be able to sue the contractor for damages resulting from defects in the work, even though the property has been transferred to a third party. The damages would be held in trust for the third party. This exception was again confirmed by the HOL in *Alfred McAlpine Construction Ltd v Panatown Ltd* [2000], in order to avoid the situation where otherwise no one would be able to sue the contractor, although on the facts the exception did not apply (because a separate arrangement had been made under which the contractor was directly liable to the third party).

ATTEMPTS TO IMPOSE OBLIGATIONS ON THIRD PARTIES

▨ Restrictive covenants inserted into a contract for the sale of land may bind subsequent purchasers, provided:

● they are negative in nature;

● the subsequent purchaser has notice of the covenants;

● the person claiming the benefit has land capable of benefiting from its enforcement (*Tulk v Moxhay* [1848]).

▨ The courts extended the rule in *Tulk v Moxhay* to personal property, for example, a ship. In *The Strathcona* [1926], the plaintiffs had chartered *The Strathcona* for certain months each year. The ship was sold to the defendant who refused to allow the plaintiffs to use the ship. The plaintiffs sought an injunction on the ground that the doctrine in *Tulk v Moxhay* should be extended from land to ships. The court granted an injunction.

This decision was criticised in *Port Line Ltd v Ben Line Ltd* [1958] where a ship chartered to the plaintiffs was sold to the defendants. The ship was requisitioned during the Suez war, and compensation was paid to the defendants. This compensation was claimed by the plaintiffs. Held – even if

The Strathcona case was rightly decided, it could not be applied in this case as (a) the defendants were not in breach of any duty and (b) the plaintiffs had sought not an injunction but financial compensation, which was outside *Tulk v Moxhay*.

The decision in *The Strathcona* has been widely criticised because:

● a contract of hire creates personal, not proprietary rights in the hired object;

● the retention of land which can benefit from the covenant is a necessary condition of the doctrine in *Tulk v Moxhay*.

However, in *Swiss Bank Corpn v Lloyds Bank* [1979], Browne-Wilkinson J considered that the decision in *The Strathcona* was correct. He suggested, however, that the tort of inducing a breach of contract or knowingly interfering with a contract would be a more suitable basis for the decision than *Tulk v Moxhay*. He stated that in his judgment a person proposing to deal with property in such a way as to cause a breach of a contract affecting that property will be restrained by injunction from doing so if, when he acquired that property, he had actual knowledge of the contract.

You should now be confident that you would be able to tick all of the boxes on the checklist at the beginning of this chapter. To check your knowledge of Privity of contract why not visit the companion website and take the Multiple Choice Question test. Check your understanding of the terms and vocabulary used in this chapter with the flashcard glossary.

Putting it into practice . . .

Now that you've mastered the basics, you will want to put it all into practice. The Routledge Questions and Answers series provides an ideal opportunity for you to apply your understanding and knowledge of the law and to hone your essay-writing technique.

We've included one exam-style essay question which replicates the type of question reproduced from the Routledge Questions and Answers series to give you some essential exam practice. The Q&A includes an answer plan and a fully worked model answer to help you recognise what examiners might look for in your answer.

QUESTION 1

Benjamin, the owner of a 1936 vintage Wolseley car, placed the following advert in the *Classic Cars Gazette:*

'For sale: 1938 Wolseley, in perfect condition, £40,000.'

Angela read the advert on Friday and telephoned Benjamin saying: 'I really want the car, but can only pay £35,000.' Benjamin said that he could not accept a penny less than £37,000 and told Angela that he would leave the offer open for a week so that she could think about it.

At 9 am the following Monday, Angela telephoned Benjamin but he was not at home, so she left a message on his answering machine saying that she would buy the car for £37,000. Later that day Claudia, Benjamin's wife, accidentally knocked the erase button on the machine before Benjamin heard the message.

That same Monday, Benjamin mentioned the Wolseley to Samuel, who immediately agreed to buy it for £40,000. The next day Samuel met Angela in their local pub and told her he had bought the car. Angela immediately went home and posted a letter to Benjamin saying she would pay the price of £37,000 that he had told her would accept the previous Friday for the Wolseley. Benjamin refused to sell her the car.

Advise Benjamin

Answer plan
This question is of a common type, raising issues about the communication of offers and acceptances, and which of two parties is entitled to enforce a

heard by Benjamin, it will not be effective. If the acceptance is effective when the message is recorded, then a contract will have come into effect on the Monday (prior to Benjamin's agreement with Samuel).

If the message on the answer machine were deemed to be a non-valid acceptance, it is necessary to deliberate the letter that Angela posted to Benjamin on the Tuesday, saying she would pay £37,000 for the Wolseley. (This of course will only be relevant if Samuel's conversation with Angela is considered not to be an effective revocation (see later)). Here, we need to consider the postal rule. The postal rule derives from the case of *Adams v Lindsell* [1818]. In this case, a letter offering some wool for sale was sent to the plaintiffs but, unfortunately, it was delayed. The plaintiffs posted a letter of acceptance as soon as they received the offer. After this letter was posted, but before it was delivered, the defendants had sold the wool elsewhere. The plaintiffs brought an action for non-delivery.

The court decided that the acceptance should be regarded as having taken effect when posted. The main reason for adopting this rule was that of business efficiency. It was thought that businesses would be able to operate more effectively if, having posted an acceptance of a contract, they could then proceed on the basis that a valid contract existed immediately, rather than having to wait to receive confirmation that the acceptance had been delivered. Later cases have confirmed that the *Adams v Lindsell* rule should apply whenever it was reasonable for the offeror to expect the acceptance to be made by post (for example, *Henthorn v Fraser* [1892]). This expectation can be removed by express instructions from the offeror (as in *Holwell Securities v Hughes* [1974], where a requirement for 'notice in writing' displaced the postal rule) or be implicit in the means of communication (for example, *Quenerduaine v Cole* [1883], where an offer by telegram was held to imply a requirement for an acceptance by equally speedy means).

From the facts given, there is no reason to suggest that the postal rule should be displaced. We should however question whether postal acceptance was reasonable, given that the offer was made verbally by telephone. Where an offer is made by instant communication, such as telex, fax or telephone, an acceptance by post would not usually be reasonable, but in this case the offer had been left open for a week which would provide ample time for a letter of acceptance to arrive. There were no specific instructions on how the acceptance was to be made. Also in *Henthorn v Fraser* [1892], where an offer was handed over in person, the court held that acceptance by post was reasonable. The discussion on whether or not the acceptance was reasonable may be rendered totally academic in the circumstances if it is found that the offer was revoked before the acceptance had taken place (see later).

Turning to the question of the revocation, we are informed that later on the Monday, Benjamin mentioned the Wolseley to Samuel, who immediately agreed to buy it for £40,000. At this stage a contract was formed between the two parties.

On Tuesday, Samuel met Angela in their local pub and told her he had bought the car. As stated earlier, an offer can generally be withdrawn at any time, notwithstanding the promise to keep it open, but revocation must be communicated. Thus it is necessary to consider whether Samuel telling Angela about the transaction in the pub would amount to revocation of Benjamin's offer. Revocation of an offer does not have to be communicated by the offeror; the communication can be acceptable if it is made by some other reliable source. Indeed the scenario in many ways replicates the course of events in *Dickinson v Dodds* [1876], which is precedent for this rule. If revocation takes place at this point, then the offer made on Friday by Benjamin will no longer be open for acceptance.

In summary, if the court decides that the answer machine message constitutes an acceptance of Benjamin's offer at £37,000, a contract will have come into play when the message was recorded. If the court takes the approach that the acceptance would only be valid when it was heard by Benjamin, then there will be no contract at this stage.

If revocation took place when Samuel informed Angela that he had purchased the car, the attempted acceptance by Angela will not be valid, due to the fact that the offer had been terminated before her acceptance. If the court finds that the revocation was not satisfactory, the court must still decide whether or not acceptance by post was reasonable, given that the offer had been made by telephone. Although it is unlikely that Angela will overcome all of these hurdles, if the court does find a valid acceptance at this stage, Benjamin will be in breach of contract if he refuses to sell to Angela. If Angela's acceptance is found to be invalid in both instances, and/or the revocation is effective, there will be no contract with Angela, but it appears that a contract has been formed between Benjamin and Samuel.

Each Routledge Q&A contains fifty essay and problem-based questions on topics commonly found on exam papers, complete with answer plans and fully worked model answers. For further examination practice, visit the Routledge website or your local bookstore today!

ROUTLEDGE Q&A SERIES

Each Routledge Q&A contains 50 questions on topics commonly found on exam papers, with comprehensive suggested answers. The titles are written by lecturers who are also examiners, so the student gains an important insight into exactly what examiners are looking for in an answer. This makes them excellent revision and practice guides.

Titles in the series include:
Business Law
Civil Liberties & Human Rights
Company Law
Commercial Law
Constitutional & Administrative Law
Contract Law
Criminal Law
Employment Law
English Legal System
Equity & Trusts
European Union Law
Evidence
Family Law
Intellectual Property Law
Jurisprudence
Land Law
Torts

For a full listing, visit:
www.routledgelaw.com/revisionaids.asp

Routledge
Taylor & Francis Group